Pocket
BALI

TOP SIGHTS • LOCAL LIFE • MADE EASY

04455200

In This Book

QuickStart Guide

Your keys to under-standing the city – we help you decide what to do and how to do it

Need to Know
Tips for a smooth trip

Regions
What's where

Explore Bali

The best things to see and do, region by region

Top Sights
Make the most of your visit

Local Life
The insider's city

The Best of Bali

The city's highlights in handy lists to help you plan

Best Walks
See the city on foot

Bali's Best...
The best experiences

Survival Guide

Tips and tricks for a seamless, hassle-free city experience

Getting Around
Travel like a local

Essential Information
Including where to stay

Our selection of the city's best places to eat, drink and experience:

◎ **Sights**

✖ **Eating**

🅟 **Drinking**

✪ **Entertainment**

🅐 **Shopping**

These symbols give you the vital information for each listing:

♪ Telephone Numbers	👪 Family-Friendly
⊙ Opening Hours	🐾 Pet-Friendly
🅟 Parking	🚌 Bus
⊘ Nonsmoking	⛴ Ferry
@ Internet Access	Ⓜ Metro
🛜 Wi-Fi Access	Ⓢ Subway
🌱 Vegetarian Selection	🚊 Tram
🗎 English-Language Menu	🚆 Train

Find each listing quickly on maps for each region:

Bar Hemingway

16 🅟 Map p233, B2

Legend has it that Hemi
self, wielding a machine
rate this timber-pan
ered bar during
showpiece is a
n by Papa ar
town. Dress
s.com; Hôtel Rit
⊙6.30pm-2a

6 ◎ *Plac*
V

Lonely Planet's Bali

Lonely Planet Pocket Guides are designed to get you straight to the heart of the city.

Inside you'll find all the must-see sights, plus tips to make your visit to each one really memorable. We've split the city into easy-to-navigate regions and provided clear maps so you'll find your way around with ease. Our expert authors have searched out the best of the city: walks, food, nightlife and shopping, to name a few. Because you want to explore, our 'Local Life' pages will take you to some of the most exciting areas to experience the real Bali.

And of course you'll find all the practical tips you need for a smooth trip: itineraries for short visits, how to get around, and how much to tip the guy who serves you a drink at the end of a long day's exploration.

It's your guarantee of a really great experience.

Our Promise

You can trust our travel information because Lonely Planet authors visit the places we write about, each and every edition. We never accept freebies for positive coverage, so you can rely on us to tell it like it is.

QuickStart Guide **7**

Explore Bali **21**

Worth a Trip:

The Best of Bali 129

Bali's Best Walks

Bali's Best...

Survival Guide 147

QuickStart Guide

Welcome to Bali

The mere mention of Bali evokes thoughts of a paradise. It's more than a place; it's a mood, an aspiration, a tropical state of mind. Bali's rich culture plays out at all levels of life, from exquisite flower-petal offerings to traditional music and dance. Add in great beaches, world-class surfing, superb dining, stunning sunsets, beautiful walks and fabulous shopping, and Bali is simply unbeatable.

Traditional Balinese dancer
KERTU / SHUTTERSTOCK ©

Bali
Top Sights

Pura Luhur Batukau (p58)

Pura Luhur Batukau, one of Bali's most important temples, never fails to touch the spirit. It is a mystical – and misty – place to contemplate Bali's beliefs and to commune with nature.

Ulu Watu's Beaches (p68)

A little plume of white sand rises out of the blue Indian Ocean and fills a cove below limestone cliffs clad in deep green tropical beauty. It sounds idyllic, and it is.

Nusa Lembongan (p90)

Lazing on a beach, riding a wave, meeting a parrotfish while snorkelling, coming face to face with a sunfish while diving in deep clear waters: these moments define Nusa Lembongan.

Touring Ubud's Rice Fields (p100)

Ribbons of green sinuously curving around hillsides crested by coconut palms and emerald patchworks blanketing the land: these are some of the vistas you'll savour as you walk Ubud's rice fields.

Gili Trawangan (p126)

An all-day, all-night party, that's Gili T – take a fast boat over from Bali to whoop it up. Divers can also find briny joy and snorkellers will discover underwater beauty right off the beach.

Bali
Local Life

Insider tips to help you find the real city

After checking out Bali's top experiences, find out what makes this magnificent island tick. Discover the beauty of sunsets from the beaches, and savour the culture and purely Balinese lifestyle in Ubud.

Beach Walk: Batubelig to Echo Beach (p48)

▶ Deserted beaches
▶ Isolated temples

At its busiest, Kuta Beach can feel like you've stumbled into a flash mob. The same goes for Legian and even Seminyak's beaches. But head north along this seemingly limitless arc of sand from Batubelig Beach and you'll leave Bali's crowds behind. It's a fascinating stroll and you'll see temples, tiny fishing encampments, crashing surf, lots of surfers, cool cafes and outcrops of upscale beach culture.

A Perfect Ubud Day (p102)

▶ Alluring shopping
▶ A cleansed body

Ubud is all about Balinese creativity and culture – but there's another Ubud that's much more inwardly focused. On this stroll you can get your body purged of poisons, fill it with healthy nourishment, adorn it with beauty and, bringing things full circle, feel the inspiration of Balinese dance. In fact, it is a good thing that Ubud is blessed with so many fine cafes, as otherwise you might find yourself so caught up in the pleasures of wandering its lanes that you'd forget to enjoy a break.

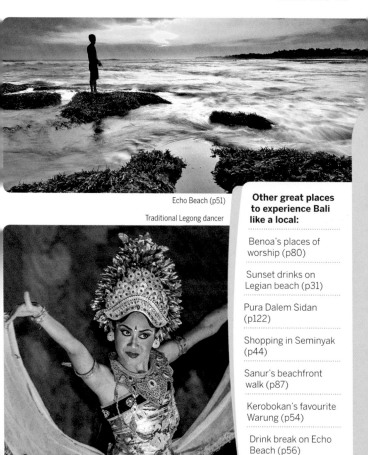

Echo Beach (p51)

Traditional Legong dancer

Other great places to experience Bali like a local:

Benoa's places of worship (p80)

Sunset drinks on Legian beach (p31)

Pura Dalem Sidan (p122)

Shopping in Seminyak (p44)

Sanur's beachfront walk (p87)

Kerobokan's favourite Warung (p54)

Drink break on Echo Beach (p56)

Ceramics showcase (p64)

Amo beauty spa (p53)

Bali
Day Planner

Day One

☀ Spend your first day in Bali's tourism heart. Begin by learning to surf Kuta Beach's reliable waves at **Pro Surf School** (p28). Or learn yoga at Kerobokan's **Jiwa Bikram** (p52). Of course, you could let others do the work at the famous Seminyak spas **Bodyworks** (p38) and **Jari Menari** (p37). No matter what, enjoy breakfast at Seminyak's **Sisterfields** (p38) or **Corner House** (p40).

☼ With the sun high overhead, hit **Kuta Beach** (p26) or **Double Six Beach** (p27). Or take shelter from the rays overhead with a little shopping in Seminyak at retailicious spots like **Souq** (p43), **Prisoners of St Petersburg** (p43) or **Drifters Surf Shop** (p44). For lunch go local at **Warung Sulawesi** (p54) or **Warung Eny** (p54).

☾ Don't miss sunset drinks in the west. Buy a beer from vendors at **Legian Beach** (p26) or go more upscale at trendy **Potato Head** (p55) or one of Seminyak's beach shacks. Dinner calls for something great in Kerobokan: classy **Sardine** (p54) or shared plates at **One Eyed Jack** (p53), followed by a little something from Bali's best gelateria, **Gusto Gelato & Coffee** (p54). Close out the night at Kuta's party that never ends, starting at **Sky Garden Lounge** (p32).

Day Two

☀ This day puts you deep into Bali's cultural soul on the island's volcanic slopes. Go early before anyone else to **Pura Luhur Batukau** (p58), where you'll find a sacred temple on the slopes of its namesake volcano. Afterwards, stop to enjoy the rice fields of Jatiluwih before driving east up and down the ridges of lush foothills to Ubud.

☼ After a morning of Balinese culture, have a healthy lunch at **Moksa** (p111) or something more traditional at **Warung Teges** (p111). In the afternoon seek serenity at **Yoga Barn** (p103) or **Taksu Spa** (p108) or do it yourself with a walk through Ubud's rice fields.

☾ One Bali experience not to be missed is a traditional dance show in Ubud. Choose your dance performance and watch the dancers go through their precise motions to the cacophony of the gamelan. Fine dinner choices include **Locavore** (p110) or one of many good places on Jl Dewi Sita. Bedtime is early in the cool mountain air; enjoy the symphony of insects as you shut your eyes.

Short on time?
We've arranged Bali's must-sees into these day-by-day itineraries to make sure you see the very best of the city in the time you have available.

Day Three

☀ Using Sanur as your hub, start in Denpasar at the markets, **Pasar Badung** (p97) and **Pasar Kumbasari** (p97), when selections are the freshest. Afterwards lay low for a bit on **Sanur Beach** (p85), maybe doing a bit of swimming in the mellow waters.

☀ Have a lunch of fresh grilled seafood at **Char Ming** (p87) or one of the places along the coast road such as Merta Sari, then swing up to the rice fields and lush green hills along the Sidemen Road. See if you can catch a glimpse of Bali's most important volcano, the often cloud-shrouded Gunung Agung. Head south to Semarapura and the historically important **Kertha Gosa** (p122).

🌙 Back in Sanur, get in some spa time at **Jamu Traditional Spa** (p28) or **Glo Day Spa & Salon** (p87), then hit Jl Tamblingan for some shopping at **A-Krea** (p89) for Bali-designed goods and **Ganesha Bookshop** (p89) for a recommended read. Wiggle your toes in the sand for dinner at **Warung Pantai Indah** (p87) or **Byrdhouse Beach Club** (p88), or go more upscale at **Three Monkeys Cafe** (p87).

Day Four

☀ Spend your day south of the airport in the many-splendoured but still compact Bukit Peninsula. In the morning, don't miss Jimbaran's **fish market** (p63), or engage with your food much more hands-on at the renowned **Bumbu Bali Cooking School** (p79). After, get soaked in the family fun of water sports at **Benoa Marine Recreation** (p81) or surf legendary breaks at Ulu Watu's beaches.

☀ Behold beautiful Balinese art in the shady **Pasifika Museum** (p79) or follow the smart set to one of the beach coves such as **Balangan** (p69), **Bingin** (p72) or **Padang Padang** (p72). Each offers cafes on the sand and fine waters for a plunge.

🌙 As the sun creates its ever-changing daily show in the west, wander through the fragrant smoke of the three main areas of Jimbaran's seafood warungs (food stalls) to find your spot for dinner or at least a sunset drink. Alternatively, head to **Pura Luhur Ulu Watu** (p71) for sunset and the **dance performance** (p75) that follows. For the best Balinese meal you'll have, consider dinner at **Bumbu Bali** (p80).

Need to Know

For more information, see Survival Guide (p147)

Currency
Rupiah (Rp)

Languages
Bahasa Indonesia and Balinese

Visas
Visas are easily obtained but can be a hassle if you hope to stay longer than 30 days.

Money
ATMs are common and it's easy to exchange money. Credit cards are accepted at more expensive establishments.

Mobile Phones
Cheap local SIM cards (from 5000Rp with no calling credit) are sold everywhere. Data speeds of 3G and faster are the norm across Bali. Any modern mobile phone will work.

Time
Indonesia Central Time (GMT/UTC plus eight hours)

Tipping
Tipping a set percentage is not expected in Bali, but if the service is good, it's appropriate to leave at least 5000Rp or 10% or more.

① Before You Go

Your Daily Budget

Budget: Less than US$80
▶ Room at guesthouse or homestay: less than US$50
▶ Cheap food and drink, meals under US$5
▶ Beaches: free

Midrange: US$80–250
▶ Room at midrange hotel: US$50–150
▶ Great night out eating and drinking: from US$20
▶ Spa treatment: US$10–40

Top end: More than US$250
▶ Room at top-end hotel or resort: over US$150
▶ Lavish evening out: over US$40
▶ Car and driver per day: US$60

Useful Websites

▶ **Bali Advertiser** (www.baliadvertiser.biz) Bali's expat journal; insider tips and good columnists.

▶ **Bali Discovery** (www.balidiscovery.com) Excellent weekly summary of news and features, plus hotel deals.

▶ **Lonely Planet** (www.lonelyplanet.com/bali) Destination information, hotel bookings, traveller forum and more.

Advance Planning

Three months before Book rooms during high season.

One month before Book rooms during shoulder season.

One week before Book top restaurants and spas during high season.

2 Arriving in Bali

Most visitors arrive in Bali via flights to Ngurah Rai International Airport. From the airport, your main choices of transport are prearranged rides through your hotel or villa, or prepaid taxis.

✈ From the Airport

Destination	Taxi Fare
Kuta	80,000Rp
Seminyak	130,000Rp
Ubud	300,000Rp

✈ At the Airport

Bali's Ngurah Rai International Airport (DPS; listed as Denpasar or Bali on travel websites) has a disappointing and poorly designed terminal. The arrivals area has ATMs and money changers. Expect long lines at customs and immigration. Accommodation services may book you into inconvenient locations.

3 Getting Around

The best way to get around is with your own transport, whether you drive, hire a driver or cycle. This gives you the flexibility to explore places that are otherwise inaccessible.

🚗 Taxi

Cheap, widely available and easy to hail in south Bali. Always insist on the meter, although most drivers will automatically use it in the daytime. Bluebird Taxis are the most reliable.

🚗 Car & Driver

Very common for longer trips and all-day touring. Can be arranged through your hotel; costs US$50 to US$60 per day.

🚶 Walking

The best way to get around the Kuta–Legian–Seminyak, Nusa Dua–Tanjung Benoa and Sanur areas (often on pleasant beachfront walkways), as well as Ubud.

🚗 Car

Car rentals are often arranged from street-side vendors. Cheap and adventurous, but you are at the mercy of Bali's traffic and it's very easy to get lost. Rent a small 4WD for around US$40 a day.

🏍 Motorbike

Cheap and easily arranged, and you can weave around traffic if you are a daredevil; can be very dangerous. Rent one for as little as US$5 a day.

🚌 Tourist Bus

Combine economy with convenience. Cheap air-con buses run on a limited network that covers Kuta–Sanur–Ubud–Padangbai.

🚲 Bicycle

Increasingly, people are touring the island by *sepeda* (bike) and many visitors are using bikes around towns and for day trips.

Bali Regions

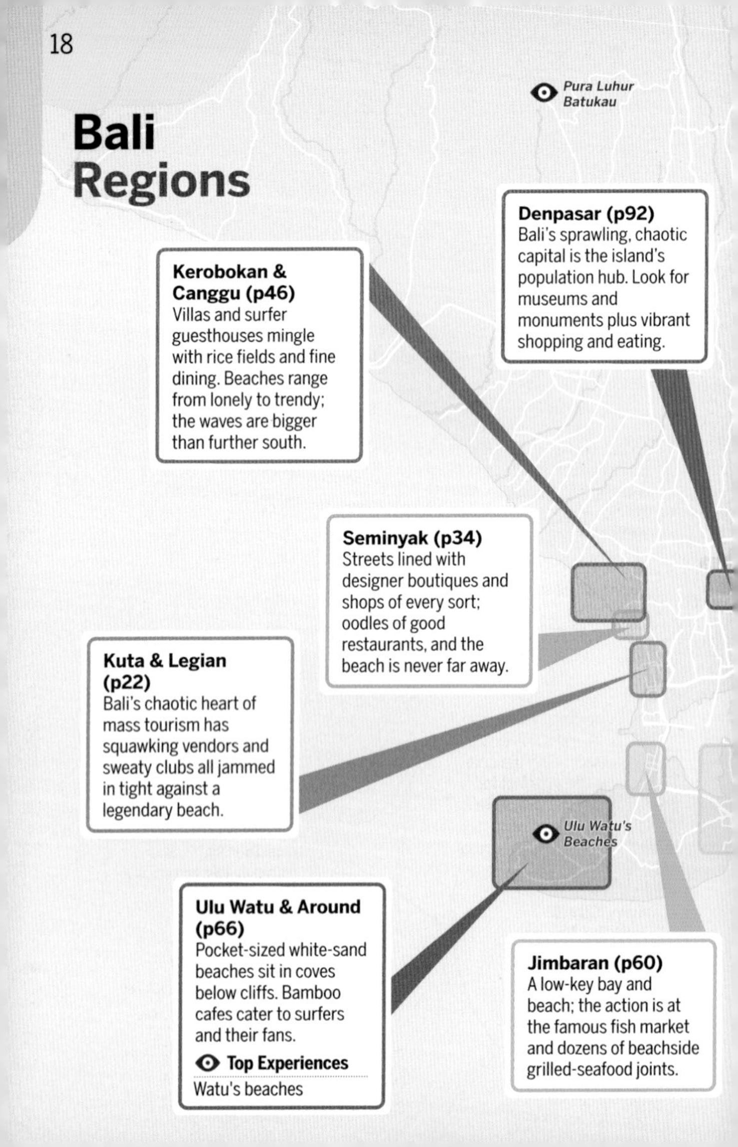

Pura Luhur Batukau

Denpasar (p92)
Bali's sprawling, chaotic capital is the island's population hub. Look for museums and monuments plus vibrant shopping and eating.

Kerobokan & Canggu (p46)
Villas and surfer guesthouses mingle with rice fields and fine dining. Beaches range from lonely to trendy; the waves are bigger than further south.

Seminyak (p34)
Streets lined with designer boutiques and shops of every sort; oodles of good restaurants, and the beach is never far away.

Kuta & Legian (p22)
Bali's chaotic heart of mass tourism has squawking vendors and sweaty clubs all jammed in tight against a legendary beach.

Ulu Watu's Beaches

Ulu Watu & Around (p66)
Pocket-sized white-sand beaches sit in coves below cliffs. Bamboo cafes cater to surfers and their fans.

⊙ Top Experiences
Watu's beaches

Jimbaran (p60)
A low-key bay and beach; the action is at the famous fish market and dozens of beachside grilled-seafood joints.

Ubud's Rice Fields

Ubud (p98)
Bali's cultural heart is an alluring mix of creative boutiques, spas and cultural performances.

⊙ Top Experiences
Touring Ubud's rice fields

Nusa Lembongan

Sanur (p82)
Combines Balinese style with a thriving expat community. The quiet beach is perfect for families too mature for Kuta.

East Bali (p118)
In the shadow of Gunung Agung, Bali's most important volcano, enjoy black-sand beaches, historic sights and impossibly green vistas.

Nusa Dua & Tanjung Benoa (p76)
Fronted by a reef-protected beach, Nusa Dua is a gated top-end resort world, while Tanjung Benoa caters to midrange groups.

Worth a Trip
⊙ Top Experiences
Pura Luhur Batukau
Nusa Lembongan
Gili Trawangan

Explore
Bali

Arts and crafts shops on Jl Dewi Sita, Ubud
MANFRED GOTTSCHALK / GETTY IMAGES ©

Explore

Kuta & Legian

Teeming, mad, crazy, wild, loud. Those are a few words that describe Kuta and Legian, the original tourist centre of Bali and the place that everyone either loves to hate or loves to love. Kuta's the original, with its narrow alleys *(gangs)*, hawkers, tawdry bars, cheap hotels and all-night clubs. Legian is pretty much the same, albeit for a slightly older crowd.

The Region in a Day

☀️ Start your day taking advantage of Bali's ever-reliable waves by learning to surf at one of the good schools such as **Pro Surf School** (p28) or **Rip Curl School of Surf** (p28). After a couple of hours in the water, join late-risers and all-nightclubbers for an early lunch. The north end of Legian offers good choices: try either **Warung Asia** (p31) or **Warung Murah** (p30).

☀️ In the afternoon, if time by the hotel pool doesn't divert you, head out for some serious beach action at **Kuta Beach** (p26), **Legian Beach** (p26) or **Double Six Beach** (p27). Or head indoors for some rejuvenating spa action at **Jamu Traditional Spa** (p28). Don't miss sunset drinks from vendors on the mellow stretch of Legian Beach.

🌙 Enjoy an elegant Balinese meal at **Poppies Restaurant** (p28) or go for Asian fusion at **Fat Chow** (p29). Now prepare for the all-night party march, the number one reason people flock to Kuta. Check the happy hour schedule and follow the crowds from one club to the next. Make **Sky Garden Lounge** (p32) your hub, with forays to surrounding venues.

 Best of Bali

Pampering
Jamu Traditional Spa (p28)

Drinking & Nightlife
Sky Garden Lounge (p32)

Double-Six Rooftop (p31)

Surfing
Kuta Beach (p26)

Double Six Beach (p27)

Pro Surf School (p28)

Rip Curl School of Surf (p28)

For Kids
Rip Curl School of Surf (p28)

Waterbom Park (p27)

Shopping
Surfer Girl (p33)

Joger (p33)

UpCycle (p33)

Luke Studer (p32)

Getting There

🚕 **Taxi** Taxis from the airport, which is just south of Kuta, will cost 40,000Rp to 60,000Rp.

🚶 **Walk** You can easily walk all of Kuta and Legian. The beach is always the most pleasant; Jl Legian is filled with aggressive vendors.

Jl Raya Kuta (Jl

Jl Nakula

Jl Sunset

Jl Dewi Sri

30

16

Sungai Mati

Jl Patih Jelantik

13

Jl Pura Puseh

Jl Nakula

24

LEGIAN

Jl Legian

Jl Melasti

Gang Abdi

Gang Camplung Mas

Jamu Traditional Spa

Jl Padma (Jl Yudistra)

Jl Sahadewa

26

31

Jl Pura Bagus Taruna
(Jl Werkudara)

Jl Padma Utara

11

Jl Arjuna (Jl Double Six)

Gang Legian
Tewogah

Jl Padma Utara

19

*Legian
Beach*

2

20

21

*Rip Curl
School
of Surf*

10

29

23

6

*Double Six
Beach*

Jl Imam Bonjol

Jl Majapahit

Jl Blambangan

Jl Raya Kuta

32

BEMO CORNER

17

7 Memorial Wall

27

33

12

Jl Leglan

28

22

Gang Bedugul

Poppies Gang I

Jl Pantai Kuta

Jl Tengal Wangi

Jl Benesari

Jl Lebak Bene (Jl Benesari)

Poppies Gang II (Jl Batu Bolong)

KUTA

Gang Sorga

Jl Bakung Sari (Jl Singasari)

Jl Kartika plaza (Jl Dewi Sartika)

Waterbom Park

8

25

Museum Kain

4

15

18

14

3

Bali Sea Turtle Society

1

Kuta Beach

Jl Pantai Kuta (Kuta Beach Rd)

5

Teluk Kuta

N

500 m
0.25 miles

Experiences

Kuta Beach
BEACH

1 Map p24, C6

Tourism in Bali began here and is there any question why? Low-key hawkers will sell you soft drinks and beer, snacks and other treats, and you can rent surfboards, lounge chairs and umbrellas (negotiable at 10,000Rp to 20,000Rp), or just crash on the sand. The sunsets are legendary.

Legian Beach
BEACH

2 Map p24, B3

An extension north from Kuta Beach, Legian Beach is quieter thanks to the lack of a raucous road next to the sand and fewer people.

Bali Sea Turtle Society
HATCHERY

3 Map p24, C7

One of the more responsible turtle hatcheries on Bali, here you can re-release turtle hatchlings into the ocean from Kuta Beach, at around 4.30pm from April to October. The release is organised by the Bali Sea Turtle Society, a conservation group working to protect olive ridley turtles. Join the queue to collect your baby turtle in a small plastic water bath, pay a small donation and join the group to release them. Signs offer excellent background info. (www.baliseaturtle.org; Kuta Beach; ⊙site 24hr, 4.30pm Apr-Oct)

Top Tip
Kuta's Famous Beaches
It's the beach that put Kuta on the map. The strand of sand stretching for more than 12km from Tuban north to Kuta, Legian and beyond to Seminyak and Echo Beach is always a scene of surfing, massaging, games, chilling, imbibing and more. Sunsets are a time of gathering for just about everyone in south Bali. When conditions are right, you can enjoy an iridescent magenta spectacle better than fireworks.

Museum Kain
MUSEUM

4 Map p24, C6

An unexpected haven of high culture in the heart of Kuta Beach, this air-con complex in the upper levels of the Beachwalk mall celebrates indigenous textiles. Exhibits include beautiful displays of batik fabrics. You'll learn how batik is made and at times be offered a chance to make your own. Interactive screens deconstruct the patterns and designs. (☏0361-846 5568; www.museumkain.org; Jl Pantai Kuta, Beachwalk; adult/child 100,000/50,000Rp; ⊙10am-8pm Tue-Sun)

Pantai Patra Jasa
BEACH

5 Map p24, B8

This hidden gem of sand is reached by a tiny access road along the fence on the north side of the airport. There's shade, a couple of tiny warungs, views of planes landing and rarely ever a

Waterbom Park

crowd. You can head north on the lovely **beach walk** to Kuta Beach.

Double Six Beach BEACH

6 Map p24, A1

The beach becomes less crowded as you go north from Legian until very popular Double Six Beach, which is alive with pick-up games of football and volleyball all day long. It's a good place to meet partying locals. Watch out for water pollution after heavy rains.

Memorial Wall MONUMENT

7 Map p24, D6

This memorial wall reflects the inter-national scope of the 2002 bombings, and people from many countries pay their respects. Listing the names of the 202 known victims, including 88 Aus-tralians and 35 Indonesians, it is start-ing to look quite weathered. Across the street, a parking lot is all that is left of the destroyed Sari Club. (Jl Legian)

Waterbom Park WATER PARK

8 Map p24, C8

This watery amusement park covers 3.5 hectares of landscaped tropical gar-dens. It has assorted water slides (22 in total including the 'Climax'), swimming pools, a FlowRider surf machine and a 'lazy river' ride. Other indulgences include a food court, a bar and a spa. (☎0361-755676; www.waterbom-bali.com; Jl

Kartika Plaza; adult/child 520,000/370,000Rp;
⏱9am-6pm)

Pro Surf School
SURFING

9 Map p24, B4

Right along Kuta Beach, this well-
regarded school has been getting
beginners standing for years. It offers
all levels of lessons, including semi-
private ones, plus gear and board
rental. There's a pool and cool cafe.
(☑0361-751200; www.prosurfschool.com; Jl
Pantai Kuta; lessons per day from 675,000Rp)

Rip Curl School of Surf
SURFING

10 Map p24, A1

Usually universities sell shirts with
their logos; here it's the other way
round: the beachwear company sponsors a school. Lessons at all levels are
given; there are special courses for
kids. It has a location for kitesurfing,
windsurfing and stand-up paddle
boarding (SUP) in Sanur. (☑0361-
735858; www.ripcurlschoolofsurf.com; Jl
Arjuna; lessons from 700,000Rp)

Jamu Traditional Spa
SPA

11 Map p24, B4

In serene surrounds at a resort hotel
you can enjoy massage in rooms that
open onto a pretty garden courtyard. If
you've ever wanted to be part of a fruit
cocktail, here's your chance – treatments involve tropical nuts, coconuts,
papayas and more, often in fragrant
baths. (☑0361-752520, 165; www.jamutradi
tionalspa.com; Jl Pantai Kuta, Alam Kul Kul; 1hr
massage from 350,000Rp; ⏱9am-7pm)

Eating

Poppies Restaurant
INDONESIAN $$

12 Map p24, D7

Opening its doors in 1973, Poppies
was one of the first restaurants to be
established in Kuta (Poppies Gang I
is even named after it). It's popular
for its elegant garden setting and a
menu of upmarket Balinese, Western
and Thai cuisine. The *rijstaffel* (selec-
tion of dishes served with rice) and
seafood is popular. (☑0361-751059;
www.poppiesbali.com; Poppies Gang I; mains
40,000-130,000Rp; ⏱8am-11pm; 🛜)

Take
JAPANESE $$

13 Map p24, D4

Flee Bali for a relaxed version of Tokyo
just by ducking under the traditional
fabric shield over the doorway at this
ever-expanding restaurant. Hyper-
fresh sushi, sashimi and more are
prepared under the keen eyes of a
team of chefs behind a long counter.
The head chef is a stalwart at the Jimbaran fish market in the early hours.
(☑0361-759745; Jl Patih Jelantik; meals
70,000-300,000Rp; ⏱11am-midnight; 🛜)

Pisgor
INDONESIAN $

14 Map p24, C8

All sorts of goodness emerges from the
ever-bubbling deep-fryers at this narrow
storefront near the airport. The *pisang
goreng* (fried bananas) are not to be
missed and you can enjoy more esoteric
fare such as *ote-ote* (vegetable cakes).
Get a mixed bag and munch away with

raw chillies for accent. (Jl Dewi Sartika; treats from 2000Rp; ⊙10am-10pm)

Fat Chow   ASIAN $$

15   🍴   Map p24, C6

A stylish, modern take on the traditional open-fronted cafe, Fat Chow serves Asian-accented fare at long picnic tables, small tables and loungers. The food is creative, with lots of options for sharing. Among the favourites: crunchy

Asian salad, pork buns, Tokyo prawns and authentic pad Thai. (📞0361-753516; www.fatchowbali.com; Poppies Gang II; mains from 60,000Rp; ⊙9am-11pm; 🛜)

Wooyoo   ICE CREAM $

16   🍴   Map p24, D3

In a hot tropical place, what is better than ice cream? The soft-serve treats here come from a well-known Korean brand renowned for its rich,

Understand
The Bali Bombings

On Saturday, 12 October 2002, two bombs exploded on Kuta's bustling Jl Legian. The first blew out the front of Paddy's Bar. A few seconds later, a far more powerful bomb obliterated the Sari Club.

The number of dead, including those unaccounted for, exceeded 200, although the exact number will probably never be known. Many injured Balinese made their way back to their villages, where, for lack of adequate medical treatment, they died.

Indonesian authorities eventually laid the blame for the blasts on Jemaah Islamiyah, an Islamic terrorist group. Dozens were arrested and many were sentenced to jail, including three who received the death penalty. But most received relatively light terms, including Abu Bakar Bashir, a radical cleric who many thought was behind the explosions. His convictions on charges relating to the bombings were overturned by the Indonesian supreme court in 2006, enraging many in Bali and Australia. (In 2011 he was sent back to prison for 15 years after a new conviction on terrorism charges.)

On 1 October 2005, three suicide bombers blew themselves up: one in a restaurant on Kuta Square and two more at beachfront cafes in Jimbaran. It was again the work of Jemaah Islamiyah, and although documents found later stated that the attacks were targeted at tourists, 15 of the 20 who died were Balinese and Javanese employees of the places bombed.

There was also justice as Umar Patek was convicted in 2012 of helping to assemble the 2002 Bali bombs and sentenced to 20 years in jail. But threats continue: in 2012 police on Bali shot dead five suspected terrorists and there were occasional arrests of suspected terrorists through 2016.

Memorial Wall (p27)

creamy swirls. Enjoy in a cup, cone or on sweet 'snail' bread. Toppings include sweet popcorn, chocolate bits and churros. The dining area has a woodsy, open style. (Jl Dewi Sri 18F; treats from 20,000Rp; ⊙10am-10pm)

Bemo Corner Coffee Shop   CAFE $

17 🍴 Map p24, D7

An attractive oasis just off the madness of Jl Legian, this sweet little open-fronted cafe serves excellent coffee drinks, smoothies and casual fare such as sandwiches and huge trad breakfasts with eggs, bacon, sausage etc. (📞0361-755305; www.facebook.com/bemocappucino; Jl Pantai Kuta 10A; mains from 40,000Rp; ⊙8am-9pm)

Ajeg Warung   BALINESE $

18 🍴 Map p24, C8

This simple stall with shady tables is right on Kuta Beach. It dishes up some of the freshest local fare you'll find in a shady location near the sand, with views of the surf. Enter the beach where Jl Pantai Kuta turns north and walk south 100m along the beach path. (📞0822 3777 6766; Kuta Beach; mains from 20,000Rp; ⊙8am-10pm)

Warung Murah   INDONESIAN $

19 🍴 Map p24, B1

Lunch goes swimmingly at this authentic warung specialising in seafood. An array of grilled fish awaits; if you prefer fowl over fin, the *sate ayam* is succulent *and* a bargain. Hugely popular at lunch; try to arrive right before noon. Don't miss the sambal. (☎0361-732082; Jl Arjuna; meals 20,000-35,000Rp; ☺8am-11pm)

Warung Asia   ASIAN $

20 ❌ Map p24, B1

Staffed by waiters cheery even by Bali standards, this popular upstairs warung serves both Indo classics and Thai fare. It gets boozy and raucous at night. (☎0361-742 0202; Jl Werkudara; mains from 35,000Rp; ☺11am-late; 🛜)

Mozzarella   ITALIAN, SEAFOOD $$

21 ❌ Map p24, B2

The best of the beachfront restaurants on Legian's car-free strip, Mozzarella serves Italian fare that's more authentic than most. Fresh fish also features; service is rather polished and there are various open-air areas for moonlit dining, plus a more sheltered dining room. A great spot for a quiet beachfront breakfast. (☎0361-751654; www.mozzarella-resto.com; Jl Padma Utara; mains 70,000-200,000Rp; ☺7am-11pm; 🛜)

Made's Warung   INDONESIAN $$

22 ❌ Map p24, D7

Made's was the original tourist warung in Kuta and its Westernised Indonesian menu has been much copied. Classic dishes such as *nasi campur* (rice served with side dishes) are served in an open-fronted setting that harks back to when Kuta's tourist hot-

spots were lit by gas lantern. (☎0361-755297; www.madeswarung.com; Jl Pantai Kuta; mains from 40,000Rp; ☺8am-11pm)

Drinking

Double-Six Rooftop   BAR

23 🚇 Map p24, A1

Sharks swimming in aquarium-lined walls, suave loungers, a commanding location and tiki torches: this ostentatious bar above the Double-Six hotel could be the villain's lair from a Bond film. Amazing sunset views are best enjoyed from the circular booths – the minimum 1,000,000Rp spend to reserve one is redeemable against food, and perfect for groups. Drinks here are pricey. (☎0361-734300; www.doublesixrooftop.com; Double Six Beach 66; ☺3-11pm; 🛜)

Q Local Life
Sunset Drinks

Bali sunsets regularly explode in stunning displays of reds, oranges and purples. Sipping a cold one while watching this free show to the beat of the surf is the top activity at 6pm. Genial local guys offer plastic chairs on the sand and cheap, cold Bintang (20,000Rp).

In Kuta, head to the car-free south end of the beach; in Legian, the best place is the strip of beach that starts north of Jl Padma and runs to the south end of Jl Pantai Arjuna.

Jenja   CLUB

24 Map p24, C1

A very slick, high-concept nightclub in the TS Suites hotel. Spread over several levels, DJs rev it up with disco, R&B, funk, soul and techno. The crowd is a mix of well-heeled locals and expats. The restaurant serves upscale fare, good for sharing. (📞0361-882 7711; www.jenjabali.com; TS Suites, Jl Nakula 18; ⏱9pm-4am Wed-Sat)

Velvet   BAR

25 Map p24, C6

The sunset views can't be beat at this large terrace bar and cafe at the beach end of the Beachwalk mall. It morphs into a club after 10pm Wednesday to Sunday. Grab a lounger for two. (📞0361-846 4928; www.vhbali.com; Jl Pantai Kuta, Beachwalk, level 3; ⏱11am-late)

Bali Beach Shack   BAR

26 Map p24, C3

A fab open-air bar which gets nightly crowds for live music and vivacious drag shows. Live music spans pop to country. (📞0819 3622 2010; www.balibeachshack.com; Jl Sahadewa; ⏱3-11pm Tue-Sun)

Sky Garden Lounge   CLUB

27 Map p24, D6

This multilevel palace of flash flirts with height restrictions from its rooftop bar where all of Kuta twinkles around you. Look for top DJs, a ground-level cafe and paparazzi-

wannabes. Possibly Kuta's most iconic club, there are hourly drink specials. Gets backpackers, drunken teens, locals on the make etc. (www.skygardenbali.com; Jl Legian 61; ⏱24hr)

Engine Room   CLUB

28 Map p24, D6

Open to the street, this lurid club features go-go dancers in cages as a come-on. As the evening progresses almost everyone dances and clothing gets shed. It's a wild party, with four venues for hedonism and music that includes hip-hop, trap and rap. (www.engineroombali.com; Jl Legian 89; ⏱4pm-4am)

Cocoon   CLUB

29 Map p24, A1

A huge pool with a view of Double Six Beach anchors this sort of high-concept club (alcohol-branded singlets not allowed!), which has parties and events around the clock. Beds, loungers and VIP areas surround the pool; DJs spin theme nights. (📞0361-731266; www.cocoon-beach.com; Jl Arjuna; ⏱10am-late)

Shopping

Luke Studer   SPORTS & OUTDOORS

30 Map p24, D2

Legendary board-shaper Luke Studer works from this large and glossy shop. Short boards, retro fishes, single fins and classic longboards are sold ready-made or custom-built. (☑0361-894 7425; www.studersurfboards.com; Jl Dewi Sri 7A; ⊙9am-8pm)

UpCycle
DESIGN

31 Map p24, B1

Old vinyl albums, drinking cans, biscuit wrappers and the like are turned into highly useful, everyday items such as purses, bags, bracelets and more. Exploring this shop feels like a treasure hunt; the goods are made in Indonesian villages. (☑0813 9674 9986; www.navehmilo.com; Jl Arjuna; ⊙10am-8pm)

Joger
GIFTS & SOUVENIRS

32 Map p24, D8

A Bali retail legend that is the most popular store in the south. Mobs come for doe-eyed plastic puppies or one of the thousands of T-shirts bearing wry, funny or simply inexplicable phrases (almost all are limited edition). In fact the sign out the front says 'Pabrik Kata-Kata', which means 'factory of words'. Warning: conditions inside the cramped store are simply insane.

When we were there the big seller said 'I love you' in a haiku of English, Chinese and Bahasa Indonesia. (☑0361-752523; Jl Raya Kuta; ⊙10am-8pm)

Surfer Girl
CLOTHING

33 Map p24, D6

A local legend, this vast store for girls of all ages has a winsome logo that says it all. Clothes, gear, bikinis and plenty of other stuff in every shade of bubblegum ever made. (☑0361-752693; www.surfer-girl.com; Jl Legian 138; ⊙9.30am-11pm)

Explore

Seminyak

Seminyak is where one talks about designers – or claims to be one. Bali's poshest shops can be found here, as can scores of top restaurants from casually fun to attitudey outdoor lounges–slash–supper clubs. World-class hotels line the beach, and what a beach it is – as wide and sandy as Kuta's but less crowded. It may be immediately north of Kuta and Legian, but Seminyak feels almost like it's on another island.

The Region in a Day

☀ Start with a leisurely late breakfast at **Sisterfields** (p38) or **Corner House** (p40). Then get yourself limbered up for the day ahead at one of Seminyak's many spas such as **Prana** (p38) or **Jari Menari** (p37). Wander over to **Seminyak Beach** (p37; pictured left): feel the salty air and pause to ponder the offerings at **Pura Petitenget** (p37).

☀ Enjoy lunch at any of many casual spots that line Seminyak's restaurant row, Jl Kayu Aya. **Revolver** (p41) and **Ginger Moon** (p39) are but two examples. Now you're ready for one of Bali's highlights: shopping in Seminyak. Top options include **Theatre Art Gallery** (p44) on Jl Raya Seminyak, **Bamboo Blonde** (p44) and **Prisoners of St Petersburg** (p43) on Jl Kayu Aya, and **Souq** (p43) on Jl Basangkasa.

☾ Enjoy a predinner drink at **Red Carpet Champagne Bar** (p42) or one of the beach bars south of Jl Abimanyu. Dinner will swamp you with choices but it's an easy walk across the sand to **La Lucciola** (p39) or inland at **Mama San** (p39). Later, party the hours away at **La Favela** (p41) or the spectacle that is **Bali Joe** (p42).

 Best of Bali

Best Drinking & Nightlife
Red Carpet Champagne Bar (p42)

La Favela (p41)

Ryoshi Seminyak House of Jazz (p41)

Bali Joe (p42)

Shopping
Milo's (p44)

Prisoners of St Petersburg (p43)

Bamboo Blonde (p44)

Thaikila (p45)

Theatre Art Gallery (p44)

Souq (p43)

Ashitaba (p45)

Drifter Surf Shop (p44)

Getting There

🚖 **Taxi** Taxis from the airport will cost 80,000Rp to 130,000Rp.

🚶 **Walk** Jl Raya Seminyak and Jl Raya Basangkasa have decent walking. Unfortunately, Jl Kayu Aya, Jl Petitenget and Jl Drupadi spell pedestrian peril. Beware blind corners and chasms that can cause great injury. When possible, opt for the beach, a quick way to Kuta and Legian.

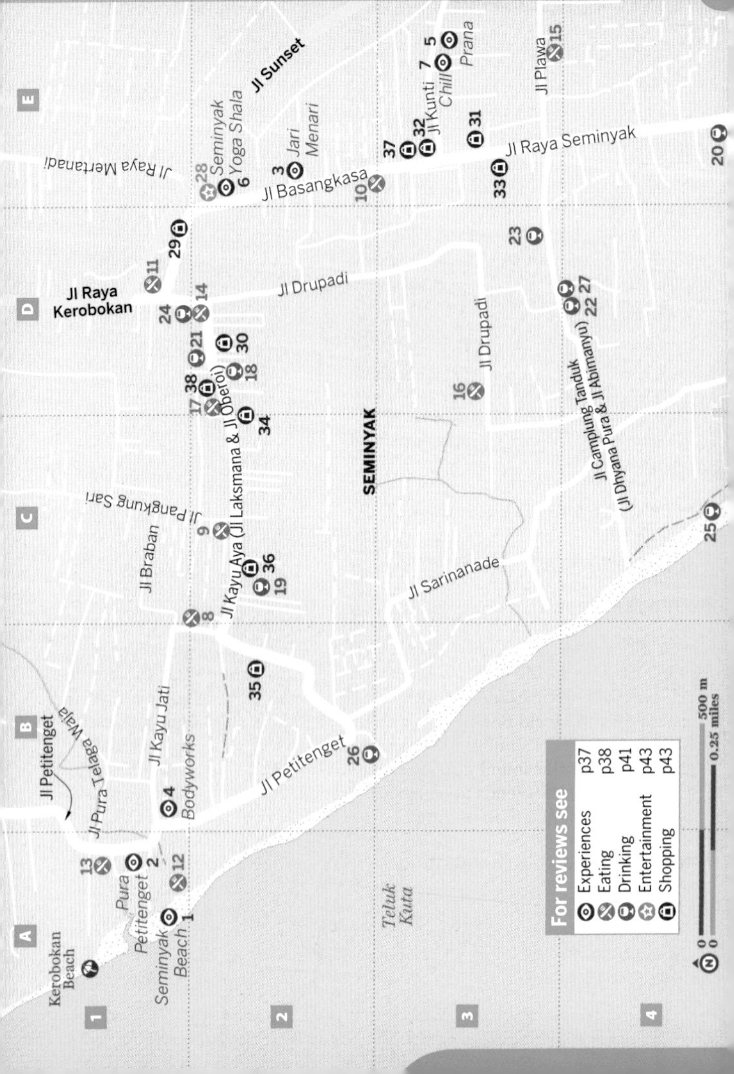

Kerobokan Beach

Jl Petitenget

Jl Pura Telaga Wala

Pura
Petitenget 2

Seminyak Beach 1

13

4

12

35

26

Jl Kayu Jati

Bodyworks

Jl Petitenget

Jl Braban

Jl Pangkung Sari

9

8

Jl Kayu Aya (Jl Laksmana & Jl Oberoi)

36
19
34
18
30
17
38
21

24

11
29

Jl Raya Kerobokan

14

Jl Drupadi

SEMINYAK

Jl Sarinanade

Jl Drupadi

16

23

25

22 27

Jl Campung Tanduk
(Jl Dhyana Pura & Jl Abimanyu)

Jl Raya Mertanadi

Jl Sunset

Seminyak Yoga Shala
28
6

Jari Menari
3

Jl Basangkasa

10

37

Jl Kunti
32
7 5
Chill

Prana

31

33

Jl Raya Seminyak

Jl Piawa
15

20

Teluk Kuta

0   500 m
0   0.25 miles

N

Beach bar on Seminyak Beach

Experiences

Seminyak Beach
BEACH

1 Map p36, A1

Seminyak continues the long sweep of beach past Kuta and Legian. A sunset lounger and an ice-cold Bintang on the beach at sunset is simply magical. A good stretch can be found near Pura Petitenget, and it tends to be less crowded than further south in Kuta.

Pura Petitenget
HINDU TEMPLE

2 Map p36, A1

This is an important temple and the scene of many ceremonies. It is one of a string of sea temples that stretches from Pura Luhur Ulu Watu on the Bukit Peninsula north to Pura Tanah Lot in western Bali. Petitenget loosely translates as 'magic box'; it was a treasured belonging of the legendary 16th-century priest Nirartha, who refined the Balinese religion and visited this site often. (Jl Petitenget)

Jari Menari
SPA

3 Map p36, E2

Jari Menari is true to its name, which means 'dancing fingers': your body will be one happy dance floor. The all-male staff use massage techniques that emphasise rhythm. They also offer classes in giving massage (from US$170). (☏ 0361-736740; www.jarimenari.com; Jl Raya

Basangkasa 47; sessions from 385,000Rp; ⏰9am-9pm)

Bodyworks   SPA

4 Map p36, B1

Get waxed, get your hair done, get the kinks rubbed out of your joints – all this and more is on the menu at this uberpopular spa in the heart of Seminyak. (☎0361-733317; www.bodyworksbali. com; Jl Kayu Jati 2; massage from 295,000Rp; ⏰9am-10pm)

Prana   SPA

5 Map p36, E3

A palatial Moorish fantasy that is easily the most lavishly decorated spa in Bali, Prana offers everything from basic hour-long massages to facials and all manner of beauty treatments. (☎0361-730840; www.pranaspabali.com; Jl Kunti 118X; massages 1hr from 510,000Rp; ⏰9am-10pm)

Top Tip
Know Your Beach

Kuta Beach morphs seamlessly into Legian, then Seminyak. Because of the limited road access, the sand in Seminyak tends to be less crowded than in Kuta. This also means that the beach is less patrolled and the water conditions are less monitored. The odds of encountering dangerous rip tides and other hazards are ever-present, especially as you head north.

Seminyak Yoga Shala   YOGA

6 Map p36, E2

No-nonsense yoga studio with daily classes in several styles including ashtanga, mysore and yin yang. (☎0361-730498; www.seminyakyogashala.com; Jl Basangkasa; classes from 120,000Rp)

Chill   SPA

7 Map p36, E3

The name says it all. This Zen place embraces reflexology; treatments include full-body pressure-point massage. (☎0361-734701; www.chillreflexology.com; Jl Kunti; treatments per hour from 225,000Rp; ⏰10am-10pm)

Surf Goddess   SURFING

Surf holidays for women that include lessons, yoga, meals and lodging in a posh guesthouse in the backstreets of Seminyak. (☎0858 997 0808; www.surfgoddessretreats.com; per week package with r from US$3000)

Eating

Sisterfields   CAFE $$

8 Map p36, C2

Trendy Sisterfields does classic Aussie breakfasts such as smashed avocado, and more-inventive dishes such as truffled oyster mushrooms with duck eggs and crispy pig ears. There are also hipster faves like pulled-pork rolls and lobster sliders. Grab a seat at a booth, the counter or in the rear courtyard. Several other good coffee cafes are nearby. (☎ 0361-738454; www.sisterfieldsbali.com; Jl Kayu Cendana 7; mains 70,000-150,000Rp; ⏰ 7am-5pm; 🛜)

Ginger Moon
ASIAN $$

9 ❌ Map p36, C2

Australian Dean Keddell is one of scores of young chefs lured to Bali to run restaurants. His creation is an appealing, airy space, with carved wood and palms. The menu features a 'Best of' list of favourites, served in portions designed for sharing and grazing. Top picks include cauliflower pizza and a special chicken curry. There's a good kids' menu. (☎ 0361-734533; www.gingermoonbali.com; Jl Kayu Aya 7; mains 70,000-160,000Rp; ⏰ 11am-midnight; 🛜 👶)

Fat Gajah
ASIAN $$

10 ❌ Map p36, E2

Fat Gajah is all about dumplings and noodles, prepared with mostly organic ingredients. They come fried or steamed with innovative fillings such as beef rendang, black-pepper crab, kimchi tuna or lemongrass lamb. There's a range of small Asian plates. The spare dining room is very appealing. (☎ 0851 0168 8212; www.fatgajah.com; Jl Basangkasa 21; dumplings 52,000-110,000Rp; ⏰ 11am-10.30pm; 🛜)

Mama San
FUSION $$

11 ❌ Map p36, D1

One of Seminyak's most popular restaurants, this stylish warehouse-sized space is split into levels, with photographs hanging from exposed brick walls. The menu has an emphasis on creative dishes from across Southeast Asia. A long cocktail list provides liquid balm for the mojito set and has lots of tropical-flavoured pours. (☎ 0361-730436; www.mamasanbali.com; Jl Raya Kerobokan 135; mains 90,000-200,000Rp; ⏰ noon-3pm & 6.30-11pm; ❄ 🛜)

La Lucciola
FUSION $$$

12 ❌ Map p36, A1

A sleek beachside restaurant with good views across a lovely lawn and sand to the surf from its 2nd-floor tables. The bar is popular with sunset-watchers, most of whom move on to dinner here. The menu is a creative melange of international fare with Italian flair. (☎ 0361-730838; Jl Petitenget; mains 120,000-400,000Rp; ⏰ 9am-11pm)

Petitenget
MODERN AUSTRALIAN $$

13 ❌ Map p36, A1

If it wasn't so hot, you could be in Paris. Soft jazz classics play at this very appealing bistro run by noted Australian chef Simon Blaby that mixes a casual terrace, bar and a more formal dining area. The menu has seasonal specials and features flavours of Europe and Asia. Everything is artfully prepared; there's a fun little kids' menu. (☎ 0361-473 3054; www.petitenget.net; Jl Petitenget 40X; mains breakfast 40,000-80,000Rp, lunch & dinner 60,000-200,000Rp; ⏰ 7am-10.30pm; 🛜)

Ku De Ta (p43)

Corner House

CAFE $$

14 🍴 Map p36, D2

With polished concrete floors, dangling light bulbs, distressed walls and vintage-style furniture, this cavernous cafe is almost a Seminyak cliché. A popular brunch spot, it does great coffee, big breakfasts, homemade sausage rolls and steak sandwiches. There's also a small shady courtyard and a relaxed, breezy upstairs dining area. (📞0361-730276; www.cornerhousebali.com; Jl Laksmana 10A; dishes 35,000-125,000Rp; ⏰7am-11pm; 🛜)

Warung Taman Bambu

BALINESE $

15 🍴 Map p36, E3

This classic warung may look simple from the street but the comfy tables are – like the many fresh and spicy dishes on offer – a cut above the norm. There's a small stand for *babi guling* (spit-roast pig) right next door. (📞0361-888 1567; Jl Plawa 10; mains from 25,000Rp; ⏰9am-10pm; 🛜)

Wacko Burger

BURGERS $$

16 🍴 Map p36, D3

It's like you died and went to comfort-food heaven. The burgers here are beloved, as are the onion rings, fries, shakes and more. There are all manner of toppings and condiments to choose from. The tables are in an open-air covered patio with actual rice-field views. (📞0821 4401 0888; www.wackoburger.com; Jl Drupadi 18; mains from 50,000Rp; ⏰noon-9.30pm)

Earth Cafe & Market

VEGETARIAN $$

17 Map p36, D2

The good vibes are organic at this vegetarian cafe and store. Choose from creative salads, sandwiches or wholegrain vegan and raw-food goodies. It's most famous for its six-course 'Planet Platter'. The beverage menu includes fresh juices and detox mixes. (0851 0304 4645; www.earthcafebali. com; Jl Kayu Aya; mains 40,000-100,000Rp; 7am-11pm;)

Drinking

La Favela

BAR

18 Map p36, D2

An alluring, mysterious entry lures you into full bohemian flair at La Favela, one of Bali's coolest and most original nightspots. Themed rooms lead you on a confounding tour from dimly lit speakeasy cocktail lounges and antique dining rooms to graffiti-splashed bars. Tables are cleared after 11pm to make way for DJs and a dance floor. (0361-730603; www.lafavela.com; Jl Kayu Aya 177X; noon-3am;)

Revolver

CAFE

19 Map p36, C2

Wander down a tiny *gang* and push through narrow wooden doors to reach this matchbox of a coffee bar that does an excellent selection of brews. There

Top Tip

are just a few tables in the creatively retro room that's styled like a Wild West saloon; nab one and enjoy tasty fresh bites for breakfast and lunch. (0361-788 4968; off Jl Kayu Aya; coffee 20,000-30,000Rp; 7am-6pm;)

Ryoshi Seminyak House of Jazz

BAR

20 Map p36, E4

The Seminyak branch of the Bali chain of Japanese restaurants has live jazz three nights a week on an intimate stage under a traditionally thatched roof. Expect some of the best local and visiting talent. (0361-731152; www.facebook.com/ryoshibali; Jl Raya Seminyak 17; noon-midnight, music from 9pm Mon, Wed & Fri)

Understand
Alcohol-Free Hangover

Nearly every tourist on Bali enjoys a drink. Thus proposals by religious conservatives in the Indonesian legislature in 2016 to ban alcohol across the nation caused a few minor strokes in Bali's tourism industry. Although the proposals were not passed, it's expected that they will resurface again. How Bali responds – both on the tourist industry side and on the cultural side (Bali's Hindus have no cultural taboo on drinking) – will be a major topic in the coming years.

Red Carpet Champagne Bar
BAR

21 Map p36, D2

Choose from more than 200 types of champagne at this over-the-top glam bar on Seminyak's couture strip. Waltz the red carpet and toss back a few namesake flutes while contemplating a raw oyster and displays of frilly frocks. It's open to the street (but elevated, darling) so you can gaze down on the masses. (☎0361-737889; www.redcarpetchampagnebar.com; Jl Kayu Aya 42; �rnoon-late)

Bali Joe
GAY & LESBIAN

22 Map p36, D4

One of several lively LGBT venues along this strip. Drag queens and go-go dancers rock the house nightly.

(☎0361-730931; www.balijoebar.com; Jl Camplung Tanduk; �3pm-3am; 🛜)

Koh
CLUB

23 Map p36, D3

Popular with locals and expats (as opposed to tourists), Koh can be quiet but it does have events with world-class DJs when it jams. Entry is through a cargo container. (☎0812 3643 9919; www.facebook.com/kohbali; Jl Camplung Tanduk; �11pm-5am Thu-Sat)

Anomali Coffee
CAFE

24 Map p36, D1

A Jakarta-based chain, Anomali is a serious coffee drinker's standout. Single-origin beans are sourced from across the archipelago and roasted on-site. Take your pick of V-60 drip coffee, Aeropress, siphon or espresso made by expert baristas in cool warehouse-style surrounds. It also sells packaged ground beans. (☎0361-767119; www.anomalicoffee.com; Jl Kayu Aya 7B; coffee from 26,000Rp; �6.30am-10pm; 🛜)

Champlung Bar
BAR

25 Map p36, C4

The most substantial of the beach bars along the beach walk south of Jl Camplung Tanduk, Champlung has its share of ubiquitous brightly coloured umbrellas and beanbags on the sand, plus a typical beach menu (pizzas, noodles etc). After sunset, expect DJs and beach parties. (☎0361-730603; off Jl Camplung Tanduk; �11am-midnight)

Ku De Ta
CLUB

26 ☻ Map p36, B2

Ku De Ta teems with Bali's beautiful people (including those whose status is purely aspirational). Scenesters perfect their 'bored' look over drinks during the day while gazing at the fine stretch of beach. Sunset brings out crowds, who dine on eclectic fare at tables. The music throbs with increasing intensity through the night. Special events are legendary. (☎0361-736969; www.kudeta.net; Jl Kayu Aya 9; ⏱8am-late; 🛜)

Bottoms Up
GAY

27 ☻ Map p36, D4

Nightly drag shows, go-go dancers and general frivolity. (www.bottomsup-seminyak.webs.com; Jl Camplung Tanduk; ⏱6pm-4am)

Entertainment

Upstairs Lounge Cinema Club
CINEMA

28 ⭐ Map p36, E2

State-of-the-art screenings of new, classic, art-house and unusual movies in a comfy and small cinema. Admission is free with any food purchase from the downstairs **Divine Earth** (www.divineearthbali.com; mains 50,000-140,000Rp; ⏱7am-11pm; ❄🛜🍴) cafe. (☎0361-731964; www.facebook.com/divineearthbali; JL Raya Basangkasa 1200A; ⏱films 8pm)

Shopping

Souq
HOMEWARES

29 🔒 Map p36, D1

The Middle East meets Asia at this glossy high-concept store with Bali-designed housewares and clothing. It has a small cafe with healthy breakfast and lunch choices plus good coffee and cold-pressed juices. (☎0822 3780 1817; www.souqstore.co; Jl Basangkasa 10; ⏱8.30am-8pm)

Prisoners of St Petersburg
FASHION & ACCESSORIES

30 🔒 Map p36, D2

Some of Bali's hottest young designers are behind this eclectic and ever-evolving hip collection of women's wear and accessories. (☎0361-736653; Jl Kaya Aya 42B; ⏱10am-10pm)

Local Life
Seminyak Village Mall
Rice fields just a few years ago, this new air-con **mall** (Map p36, B2; ☎0361-738097; www.seminyakvillage.com; Jl Kayu Jati 8; ⏱9am-10pm; 🛜) deserves a compliment for being discreetly placed back from the street. The selection of shops is refreshingly local, with some notable names such as Lily Jean on the three levels. The small carts leased to up-and-coming Balinese designers is a nice touch.

Local Life
Shopping in Seminyak

Seminyak has it all: designer boutiques (Bali has a thriving fashion industry), retro-chic stores, slick galleries, wholesale emporiums and family-run workshops.

The best shopping starts on Jl Raya Seminyak at Bintang Supermarket and runs north through Jl Basangkasa. The retail strip branches off into Jl Kayu Aya and Jl Kayu Jati while continuing north on Jl Raya Kerobokan into Kerobokan. Try not to step into one of the yawning pavement caverns.

For help navigating the myriad shops, contact the singularly named Marilyn (www.retailtherapy bali.com), who brings a veteran retailer's keen eye to the local scene and offers custom shopping tours.

Indivie   ARTS & CRAFTS

31 🔒 Map p36, E3

The works of young designers based in Bali are showcased at this intriguing and glossy boutique. (☎0361-730927; www.indivie.com; Jl Raya Seminyak, Made's Warung; ⏰9am-9pm)

Samsara   CLOTHING

32 🔒 Map p36, E3

Balinese-made textiles using global inspiration. This appealing shop displays hand-painted batik used in a range of exquisite casual wear by designer Coretta Hutson. (www.samsaraboutique.com; Jl Raya Seminyak; ⏰10am-10pm)

Theatre Art Gallery   ARTS & CRAFTS

33 🔒 Map p36, E3

Specialises in vintage and reproduction *wayang* puppets used in traditional Balinese theatre. Just looking at the animated faces peering back at you is a delight. (Jl Raya Seminyak; ⏰9am-8pm)

Bamboo Blonde   CLOTHING

34 🔒 Map p36, C2

Shop for frilly, sporty or sexy frocks and formal wear at this cheery designer boutique (one of 11 island-wide). All goods are designed and made on Bali. (☎0361-731864; www.bambooblonde.com; Jl Kayu Aya 61; ⏰10am-10pm)

Milo's   CLOTHING

35 🔒 Map p36, B2

The legendary local designer of silk finery has a lavish shop in the heart of designer row. Look for batik-bearing, eye-popping orchid patterns. (☎0361-822 2008; www.milos-bali.com; Jl Kayu Aya 992; ⏰10am-8pm)

Drifter Surf Shop   FASHION & ACCESSORIES

36 🔒 Map p36, C2

High-end surf fashion, surfboards, gear, cool books and brands such as Obey and Wegener. Started by two savvy surfer dudes, the shop stocks goods noted for their individuality and high quality. There's also a small cafe-bar and a patio. (☎0361-733274; www.driftersurf.com; Jl Kayu Aya 50; ⏰7.30am-11pm)

Shop in Seminyak

Ashitaba   ARTS & CRAFTS

37 🔒 Map p36, E3

Tenganan, the Aga village of east
Bali, produces the intricate and
beautiful rattan items sold here.
Containers, bowls, purses and more
(from 50,000Rp) display the very fine
weaving. (📞0361-737054; Jl Raya Seminyak
6; 🕑9am-9pm)

Thaikila   CLOTHING

38 🔒 Map p36, D2

'The dream bikini of all women' is the
motto of this local brand that makes
a big statement with its tiny wear.
The swimwear is French-designed
and made right in Bali. If you need
something stylish for the beach, come
here. (📞0361-731130; www.blue-glue.com;
Jl Kayu Aya; 🕑9am-9pm)

Explore

Kerobokan & Canggu

Kerobokan can rightly be called Seminyak North. Jl Petitenget seamlessly links the pair and, like its southern neighbour, Kerobokan has an ever-more alluring collection of shops and some of Bali's very best restaurants. This is also ground zero for private villa rentals, with walled compounds stretching west with the coast past villa-dotted Canggu to the rugged surf and idyllic pleasures of Echo Beach (pictured above).

The Region in a Day

☀ Start your day off with you! Try some yoga at **Jiwa Bikram** (p52) or a new look at **Amo Beauty Spa** (p53). Go for an invigorating ride on the surf breaks at **Batu Bolong Beach** (p51). Lighten your wallet while filling the carry-on at any of many fine housewares stores such as **Hobo** (p57), or save money and space at the kid-friendly **JJ Bali Button** (p57).

☼ Kerobokan has a number of simple warungs that showcase Indonesian foods in settings visitors will enjoy; try **Warung Sulawesi** (p54) or **Warung Goûthé** (p53). For the afternoon, find your perfect spot of sand at the increasingly popular **Batubelig Beach** (p51), or Echo Beach, where you'll find sunbed and drink vendors. Or go for one of the less-visited stretches of sand on either side of Batu Bolong Beach.

☽ Look for a venue that grabs your fancy for sunset views at Batubelig Beach, just west of Kerobokan. Then don your nice duds and choose from some of Bali's best drinking and dining at **Sardine** (p54), or try tasty **Warung Eny** (p54).

For a local's day in Kerobokan & Canggu, see p48.

 Best of Bali

Beaches
Batu Bolong Beach (p51)

Echo Beach (p51)

Nightlife
Black Shores (p55)

Potato Head (p55)

Pampering
Sundari Day Spa (p51)

Eating
Sardine (p54)

Warung Goûthé (p53)

Warung Sulawesi (p54)

Warung Eny (p54)

Shopping
JJ Bali Button (p57)

Hobo (p57)

Bathe (p56)

Dylan Board Store (p57)

Getting There

🚕 **Taxi** Taxis from the airport will cost 100,000Rp to 225,000Rp.

This area is quite spread out; even walks to the beach might be 2km or more. Renting a scooter, taking a taxi or getting rides from your villa driver will be necessary. Echo Beach has a taxi stand.

Local Life
Beach Walk: Batubelig to Echo Beach

Walking the beach, it's only 4km from Batubelig Beach to Echo Beach, compared with a long circuitous drive inland. You'll cover stretches of empty sand and ford streams with only the roar of the surf for company. A few villages, temples, villas and simple cafes provide interest away from the water. You'll get wet on this walk; bring a waterproof bag for valuables.

❶ Batubelig Beach

Start this walk at one of the beach bars and cafes along Batubelig Beach. Get your fluids in for an adventure that can take anywhere from an hour to half a day depending on your whim. Look northwest along the beach and you can see the developments at Echo Beach in the distance.

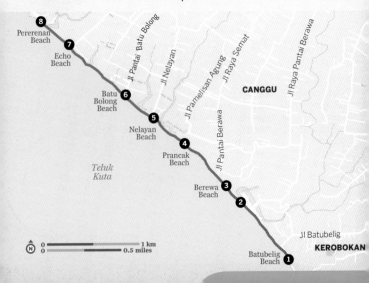

❷ Water Crossing

The biggest obstacle on this entire walk is only about 500m from the start. The river and lagoon here flow into the ocean, often at a depth of 1m but at times not at all. However, after rains it may be much deeper and you'll decide not to swim the current: in this case, take the cool little footbridge over the lagoon to the groovy outdoor lounge La Laguna, where you can call for a taxi.

❸ Berawa Beach

Now one of Canggu's hip centres, this stretch of beach has a high-concept Finn's Beach Club and is about 2km up the sand from Seminyak (where you can also begin this walk). There are also low-key beer vendors by the pounding sea; the grey volcanic sand here slopes steeply into foaming water. Look along the sand's edge for the vast Marabito Art Villa, a private estate that's an architectural wonder.

❹ Prancak Beach

Almost 1km further on you'll come to another (shallow) water crossing that also marks the large complex of Pura Dalem Prancak. Vendors offer drinks and surfboard rental on Pantai Prancak; turn around facing the way you've come and you can see the sweep of the beach all the way to the airport.

❺ Nelayan Beach

A collection of fishing boats and huts marks this relatively mellow stretch of sand that lacks easy access to the raw energy of Canggu just inland.

❻ Batu Bolong Beach

Hip and popular Batu Bolong Beach boasts the large Pura Batumejan complex with a striking pagodalike temple. There are surfboard rentals, cafes such as the legendary hang-out Old Man's and a vibrant mix of people. Drink vendors service loungers on the sand.

❼ Echo Beach

Construction along the shore means you've reached Echo Beach, where you can reward yourself for your adventurous walk at the many cafes. A flock of shops means you can replace any clothes that are drenched beyond repair. Otherwise, take your camera out of its waterproof bag and nab shots of the popular surf break.

❽ Pererenan Beach

Going west from Echo Beach is the region's next hotspot, Pererenan Beach. It's an easy 300m further on from Echo Beach via sand and rock formations. You'll be spoiled for drinks and food by the dozen ephemeral bamboo joints built right on the sand. But all that's needed is one developer to sneeze and they'll all be gone.

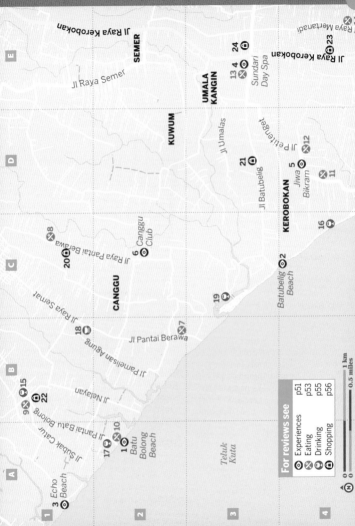

SEMER

Jl Raya Kerobokan

Jl Raya Semer

UMALA
KANGIN

KUWUM

Jl Umalas

24 🏠

13 4 ❌
Sundari
Day Spa

Jl Raya Kerobokan

23 🏠

Jl Raya Mertanadi

14 ❌

21 🏠

Jl Petitenget

Jl Batubelig

12 ❌

KEROBOKAN

Jiwa
Bikram

5 🏠

11 ❌

8 ❌

20 🏠

Jl Raya Pantai Berawa

6 Canggu
Club 🏠

CANGGU

16 🏠

Batubelig
Beach 🏠 2

19 ❌

Jl Raya Semat

18 🏠

Jl Pamelisan Agung

7 🏠

Jl Pantai Berawa

15 🏠

9 ❌

🏠 22

Jl Nelayan

Jl Pantai Batu Bolong

Jl Subak Catu

17 ❌

10 ❌
1 🏠

Batu
Bolong
Beach

Teluk
Kuta

3 Echo 🏠
Beach

For reviews see	
🏠 Experiences	p51
❌ Eating	p53
🏠 Drinking	p55
🏠 Shopping	p56

0   1 km
0   0.5 miles

Ⓝ

KONSTANTIN TRUBAVIN / ALAMY STOCK PHOTO ©

Batu Bolong Beach

Experiences

Batu Bolong Beach BEACH

1 Map p50, A2

The beach at Batu Bolong is the most popular in the Canggu area. There's almost always a good mix of locals, expats and visitors hanging out in the cafes, surfing the breaks or watching it all from the sand. There are rental loungers, umbrellas and beer vendors.

Batubelig Beach BEACH

2 Map p50, C4

The sand narrows here but there are some good places for a drink, both grand and simple. Easily reached via Jl Batubelig, this is a good place to start a walk along the curving sands northwest to popular beaches as far as Echo Beach.

Echo Beach BEACH

3 Map p50, A1

Surfers and those who like to watch them flock here for the high-tide left-hander that regularly tops 2m. The greyish sand right in front of the developments can vanish at high tide, but you'll find wide strands east and west. Batu Bolong Beach is 500m east.

Sundari Day Spa SPA

4 Map p50, E3

This much-recommended spa strives to offer the services of a five-star resort without the high prices. The massage

Understand
The Villa Life

Villas are scattered around south Bali and Ubud, and are now appearing in the east. They're often built in the middle of rice paddies, seemingly overnight. The villa boom has been quite controversial for environmental, aesthetic and economic reasons. Many skip collecting government taxes from guests, which has raised the ire of their luxury hotel competitors and brought threats of crackdowns.

Large villas can be bacchanalian retreats for groups of friends, such as those found in the Canggu area. Others are smaller, more intimate and part of larger developments – common in Seminyak and Kerobokan – or top-end hotels. Expect the following: a private garden and pool; a kitchen; air-con bedroom(s); and an open-air common space. Villas will also potentially include your own staff (cook, driver, cleaner), a private beachfront and isolation (which can be good or bad).

Rates range from under US$200 per night for a modest villa to US$2000 per week and beyond for your own tropical estate. There are often deals, especially in the low season, and several couples sharing can make something grand affordable. You can sometimes save quite a bit by waiting until the last minute, but during the high season the best villas book up far in advance.

It's the Wild West out there. There are myriad agents, some excellent, others not. It is essential to be as clear as possible about what you want, and what exactly is included in the fee, when arranging a rental.

Local agents include **Bali Discovery** (☏0361-286283; www.balidiscovery.com), **Bali Private Villas** (☏0361-844 4344; www.baliprivatevillas.com) and **Bali Ultimate Villas** (☏0851 0057 1658; www.baliultimatevillas.net).

---

oils and other potions are organic, and there's a full menu of therapies and treatments on offer. (☏0361-735073; www.sundari-dayspa.com; Jl Petitenget 7; massages from 250,000Rp; ⏱10am-10pm)

Jiwa Bikram   YOGA

 5 Map p50, D4

In a convenient location, this no-frills place offers several different types of yoga, including bikram, hot

flow and yin. (☏0361-841 3689; www.jiwabikram.com; Jl Petitenget 78; classes from 180,000Rp; ⏱9am-8pm)

Canggu Club   HEALTH & FITNESS

6 Map p50, C2

Bali's expats shuttlecock themselves silly at the Canggu Club, a New Age version of something you'd expect to find during the Raj. The vast, perfectly virescent lawn is manicured for croquet. Get sweaty with tennis, squash, polo, cricket, bowling, the spa or the 25m pool. Many villa rentals include guest passes here. The garish **Splash Waterpark** is popular. (☑0361-848 3939; www.cangguclub.com; Jl Pantai Berawa; adult/child day pass 300,000/180,000Rp; ☻6am-10pm)

Eating

One Eyed Jack   JAPANESE $$

7 🍴 Map p50, B2

Izakaya, the style of Japanese dining that encourages groups of friends to enjoy drinks and shared plates of food, is exemplified by this wonderful small restaurant. The chef is a veteran of internationally acclaimed Nomu; the dishes are superb. Tiny taco-style appetisers, chicken *tsukune* sliders and barbecue-pork buns will have you ordering seconds. Don't miss the tea-based cocktails. (☑0819 9929 1888; www.oneeyedjackbali.com; Jl Pantai Berawa; ☻5pm-midnight)

Warung Goûthé   BISTRO $$

8 🍴 Map p50, C1

Superbly prepared and presented casual meals are the hallmark of this open-front cafe. The very short menu changes each day depending on what's fresh. The French owners can take a simple chicken sandwich and elevate it to magnificent and memorable. The desserts alone should cause you to stop in whenever you are nearby.

Local Life
Amo Beauty Spa

With some of Asia's top models lounging about **Amo Beauty Spa** (Map p50, D4; ☑0361-473 7943; www.amospa.com; Jl Petitenget 100X; massages from 220,000Rp; ☻9am-9pm), it feels like you've stumbled into a *Vogue* shoot. In addition to massages, services range from haircare to pedicures and unisex waxing. Book ahead.

(☑0878 8947 0638; www.facebook.com/warunggouthe; Jl Pantai Berawa 7A; mains from 60,000Rp; ☻9am-5pm Mon-Sat)

Deus Ex Machina   CAFE $$

9 🍴 Map p50, B1

This surreal venue amid Canggu's rice fields has many personas. If you're hungry it's a restaurant-cafe-bar; for shoppers it's a fashion label; if you're into culture it's a contemporary-art gallery; for music lovers it's a live-gig venue (Sunday afternoons) for local punk bands; for bikers it's a custom-made motorcycle shop; if you want your beard trimmed, it's a barber... (Temple of Enthusiasm; ☑0811 388 150; www.deuscustoms.com; Jl Batu Mejan 8; mains 60,000-170,000Rp; ☻7am-11pm; 🛜)

Old Man's   INTERNATIONAL $$

10 🍴 Map p50, A2

You'll have a tough time deciding just where to sit down to enjoy your drink at this popular coastal beer garden overlooking Batu Bolong Beach. The self-serve menu is aimed at surfers and surfer-wannabes: burgers, pizza, fish and chips, salads. Wednesday nights are an institution, while Fridays (live rock and roll) and Sundays (DJs) are also big. (0361-846 9158; www.oldmans.net; Jl Pantai Batu Bolong; mains from 50,000Rp; 8am-midnight)

Saigon Street
VIETNAMESE $$

11 Map p50, D4

Modern, vibrant and packed, this Vietnamese restaurant lures in the buzzing masses with its swanky neon decor. Creative Vietnamese dishes include peppery betel leaves filled with slow-cooked octopus, an impressive rice-paper roll selection, along with curries, pho and grilled meats cooked on aromatic coconut wood. Cocktails include the 'bang bang' mar-

Local Life
Kerobokan's Favourite Warung

Although seemingly upscale, Kerobokan is blessed with many a fine place for a truly authentic local meal. One of the very favourites is **Warung Sulawesi** (Map p50, D3; Jl Petitenget; meals from 35,000Rp; 7am-8pm). Here you'll find a table in a quiet family compound and enjoy fresh Balinese and Indonesian food served in classic warung style. Choose rice, then pick from a captivating array of dishes that are always at their peak at noon. The long beans – yum!

tini, a chilled bit of boozy splendour. Book ahead. (0361-897 4007; www.saigonstreetbali.com; Jl Petitenget 77; mains 50,000-175,000Rp; 11.30am-11pm;)

Warung Eny
BALINESE $

12 Map p50, D4

The eponymous Eny cooks everything herself at this tiny open-front warung nearly hidden behind various potted plants. Look for the roadside sign that captures the vibe: 'The love cooking'. The seafood, such as prawns smothered in garlic, is delicious and most ingredients are organic. Ask about Eny's excellent cooking classes. (0361-473 6892; www.warungeny.blogspot.com; Jl Petitenget 97; mains from 35,000Rp; 8am-11pm)

Sardine
SEAFOOD $$$

13 Map p50, E3

Seafood fresh from the famous Jimbaran market is the star at this elegant yet intimate, casual yet stylish restaurant. It's in a beautiful bamboo pavilion, with open-air tables overlooking a private rice field patrolled by Sardine's own flock of ducks. The inventive bar is a must and stays open until 1am. The menu changes to reflect what's fresh. Booking is vital. (0811 397 8111; www.sardinebali.com; Jl Petitenget 21; meals US$20-50; 11.30am-4pm & 6-11pm;)

Gusto Gelato & Coffee
GELATERIA $

14 Map p50, E4

Bali's best gelato is made fresh throughout the day, with unique

Sardine

flavours such as rich Oreo, surprising and delicious tamarind and *kamangi* (lemon basil). The classics are here as well. It gets mobbed in the afternoons. (☏0361-552 2190; www.gusto-gelateria.com; Jl Raya Mertanadi 46; gelato from 22,000Rp; ☺10am-10pm; ✳☺)

Drinking

Black Shores   BAR

15 🚇 Map p50, B1

A laid-back bar with a pure Canggu vibe. Creative bartenders concoct drinks that are boozy, fresh and often fruity. Regular live acts (usually Friday nights) feature top visiting bands. When crowded it feels like a big house party by the beach, which it sort of is. (☏0813 3987 4055; Jl Batu Bolong; ☺4pm-midnight)

Potato Head   CLUB

16 🚇 Map p50, C4

Bali's highest-profile beach club is one of the best. Wander up off the sand or follow a long drive off Jl Petitenget and you'll find much to amuse, from an enticing pool to a swanky restaurant, plus lots of loungers and patches of lawn for chillin' the night away under the stars. (☏0361-473 7979; www.ptthead.com; Jl Petitenget; ☺11am-2am; ☺)

Ji
BAR

17 Map p50, A2

Easily Canggu's most alluring bar, Ji is a fantasy of historic Chinese and Balinese woodcarving and rich decor. From the terrace on the 1st floor, there are fine views you can enjoy with exotic cocktails, sake and Japanese bites. (☑0361-473 1701; www.jiatbalesutra.com; Jl Pantai Batu Bolong, Hotel Tugu Bali; ⏱5-11pm)

Hungry Bird
CAFE

18 Map p50, B1

One of the few genuine third-wave coffee roasters in Bali, Hungry Bird does superb single-origin brews. The Javanese owner is incredibly knowledgeable on the subject, and roasts beans on-site from all over Indonesia; cupping sessions are possible if you call ahead. The food's also excellent (organic eggs and baked goods) and

Local Life
Drink Break on Echo Beach

Enjoying a drink while watching the surf break is an Echo Beach tradition. Just west of the main cafe cluster, a string of ephemeral beach bars have appeared that are little more than bamboo shacks. They offer beanbags on the sand and cold beer. Note that an upscale development could sweep them away overnight.

perfect for brunch. (☑0898 619 1008; www.facebook.com/hungrybirdcoffee; Jl Raya Semat 86; ⏱8am-5pm Mon-Sat; 🛜)

La Laguna
COCKTAIL BAR

19 Map p50, C3

A sibling of Seminyak's La Favela, La Laguna is one of Bali's most alluring bars. It combines a beatnik look with Moorish trappings and sparkling tiny lights. Explore the eclectic layout, and sit on a couch, a sofa bed, at a table inside or a picnic table in the garden. The drinks are good, the food is fair (mains from 75,000Rp). (☑0812 3638 2272; www.facebook.com/lalagunabali; Jl Pantai Kayu Putih; ⏱11am-midnight; 🛜)

Shopping

It Was All a Dream
FASHION & ACCESSORIES

20 Map p50, C1

Great-quality leather bags, fun sunglasses, vintage jeans, jersey basics, embroidered kaftans and more. This hip boutique has original pieces at reasonable prices. It's run by a French-American pair of expat designers. (☑0811 388 3322; Jl Pantai Berawa 14B; ⏱10am-7pm)

Bathe
BEAUTY, HOMEWARES

21 Map p50, D3

Double-down on your villa's romance with handmade candles, air diffusers, aromatherapy oils, bath salts and

Understand
Warungs

- -

The most common place for dining out in Bali is a warung, the traditional street-side eatery. There's one every few metres in major towns, and several even in small villages. They are cheap, no-frills hang-outs with a relaxed atmosphere; you may find yourself sharing a table with strangers as you watch the world go by. The food is fresh and different at each, and is usually displayed in a glass cabinet at the entrance where you can create your own *nasi campur* (rice served with side dishes) or just order the house standard.

Both Seminyak and Kerobokan in particular are blessed with numerous warungs that are visitor-friendly, but many are on offer across Bali and half the fun is finding your own favourite.

homewares that evoke the feel of a 19th-century French dispensary. It's in a cluster of upscale boutiques. (📞0811 388 640; www.bathestore.com; Jl Batu Belig 88; ◷7am-10pm)

Dylan Board Store
SPORTS & OUTDOORS

22 🔒 Map p50, B1

Famed big-wave rider Dylan Longbottom runs this custom surfboard shop. A talented shaper, he creates boards for novices and pros alike. He also stocks plenty of his own designs that are ready to go. (📞0819 9982 5654; www.dylansurfboards.com; Jl Pantai Batu Bolong; ◷10am-8pm)

Hobo
HOMEWARES

23 🔒 Map p50, E4

Elegance mixes with quirky at this enticing shop filled with gifts and housewares, most of which can slip right into your carry-on bag. (📞0361-733369; www.thehobostore.com; Jl Raya Kerobokan 105; ◷9am-8pm)

JJ Bali Button
ARTS & CRAFTS

24 🔒 Map p50, E3

Zillions of beads and buttons made from shells, plastic, metal and more are displayed in what at first looks like a candy store. Elaborately carved wooden buttons cost 800Rp. Kids may have to be bribed to leave. (Jl Gunung Tangkuban Perahu; ◷9am-5pm)

Top Sights
Feeling Spiritual at Pura Luhur Batukau

Getting There

🚗 **Car** You'll need to charter a car and driver for the day. Getting here from south Bali can take one to two hours, depending on traffic.

One of the island's holiest and most underrated temples, Pura Luhur Batukau makes for an excellent day trip and is the most spiritual temple you can easily visit. It is surrounded by forest, the atmosphere is cool and misty, and the chants of priests are backed by singing birds. The temple is near the base of Gunung Batukau, the island's second-highest mountain (2276m) and the third of Bali's three major volcanoes. Nearby, you can drive through the lushly iconic Jatiluwih rice fields.

Don't Miss

Pura Luhur Batukau

Within the temple complex, look for the seven-roofed *meru* dedicated to Maha Dewa, the mountain's guardian spirit, as well as shrines for Bratan, Buyan and Tamblingan lakes. The main *meru* in the inner courtyard have little doors shielding small ceremonial items. It's impossible to ignore the deeply spiritual mood.

Facing the temple, take a short walk around to the left to see a small white-water stream where the air resonates with tumbling water. Get here early for the best chance of seeing the dark and foreboding slopes of the volcano.

Gunung Batukau

At Pura Luhur Batukau you are fairly well up the side of Gunung Batukau. For the trek to the top of the 2276m peak, you'll need a guide, which can be arranged at the temple ticket booth. Expect to pay more than 1,000,000Rp for a muddy and arduous journey that will take at least seven hours in one direction. The rewards are amazing views alternating with thick, dripping jungle.

Jatiluwih Rice Fields

At Jatiluwih, which means 'truly marvellous' (or 'real beautiful' depending on the translation), you will be rewarded with vistas of centuries-old rice terraces that exhaust your ability to describe green. Emerald ribbons curve around the hillsides, stepping back as they climb to the blue sky.

The terraces are part of Bali's emblematic – and Unesco-recognised – ancient rice-growing culture. You'll understand the nomination just viewing the panorama from the narrow 18km road, but getting out for a rice-field walk is even more rewarding, following the water as it runs through channels and bamboo pipes from one plot to the next.

---

adult/child
20,000/10,000Rp

🕑 8am-6pm

☑ Top Tips

▶ Sashes and sarongs are provided.

▶ Admire the many forms of offerings from a few flower petals in a banana leaf to vastly elaborate affairs that can feed many gods.

▶ A two-hour mini jaunt up Batukau costs 200,000Rp.

▶ There is a road toll for Jatiluwih visitors (15,000Rp per person, plus 5000Rp per car).

▶ Much of the rice you'll see is traditional, rather than the hybrid versions grown elsewhere on the island. Look for heavy short husks of red rice.

✖ Take a Break

There are a couple of simple cafes for refreshments along the Jatiluwih drive. They are nothing fancy but you're there for the views.

Explore

Jimbaran

Just south of Kuta and the airport, Teluk Jimbaran (Jimbaran Bay; pictured above) is an alluring crescent of white-sand beach and blue sea, fronted by a long string of seafood warungs. By day, Jimbaran has two markets that bustle with business as Bali's rich stocks of fish, fruit and vegetables are bought and sold. Despite increased popularity, Jimbaran remains a relaxed alternative to Kuta and Seminyak.

The Region in a Day

Waking with the sun in Jimbaran will be rewarded when you visit the frenetic world of the **fish market** (p63), as well as the fruit and vegetable wonderland that is the **morning market** (p63). For a pause, you might try a cafe in one of the resorts that are discreetly set back from the beach.

Your afternoon should be all about Jimbaran's excellent **beach** (p63). Stroll its 4km and find a good shady spot to relax on a rented sun lounger. Despite rumours of future plans, the area is not overwhelmed yet with hotels and resorts so you won't find the sands crowded.

As the sun creates its spectacular vermilion theatrics in the west, wander through the fragrant smoke of the three main areas of seafood warungs to find your spot for dinner. The fish is always fresh from the market and you can choose from what's on offer in huge tanks and beds of ice before it goes on the flaming coconut-shell-fuelled grills.

 Best of Bali

Beaches
Jimbaran Beach (p63)

Eating
Jimbaran Fish Market (p63)

Getting There

🚕 **Taxi** Plenty of taxis wait around the beachfront warungs in the evening to take diners home (about 140,000Rp to Seminyak). Some of the seafood warungs provide free transport if you call first.

🚌 **Bus** The Kura-Kura tourist bus (www.kura2bus.com) has a route linking Jimbaran with its Kuta hub. Buses run every 75 minutes and cost 40,000Rp.

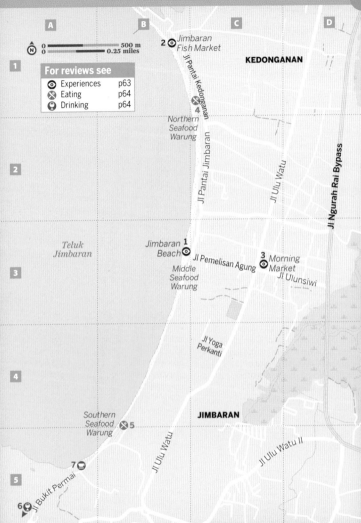

A

B

C

D

N

0   500 m
0   0.25 miles

For reviews see

⦿ Experiences   p63
❌ Eating   p64
🍷 Drinking   p64

2 ⦿ Jimbaran
Fish Market

KEDONGANAN

Jl Pantai Kedonganan

❌ 4

*Northern
Seafood
Warung*

Jl Pantai Jimbaran

Jl Ulu Watu

Jl Ngurah Rai Bypass

*Teluk
Jimbaran*

Jimbaran 1
Beach ⦿
Jl Pemelisan Agung

3 ⦿ Morning
Market

*Middle
Seafood
Warung*

Jl Ulunsiwi

Jl Yoga
Perkanti

*Southern
Seafood
Warung*

❌ 5

JIMBARAN

Jl Ulu Watu

Jl Ulu Watu II

7 🍷

6 🍷

Jl Bukit Permal

Jimbaran Fish Market

Experiences

Jimbaran Beach   BEACH

1   ⊙ Map p62, B3

One of Bali's best beaches, Jimbaran's 4km-long arc of sand is mostly clean and there is no shortage of places to get a snack, a drink, a seafood dinner or to rent a sunlounger. The bay is protected by an unbroken coral reef, which keeps the surf more mellow than at popular Kuta further north, although you can still get breaks that are fun for bodysurfing.

Jimbaran Fish Market   MARKET

2   ⊙ Map p62, B1

A popular morning stop on a Bukit Peninsula amble, this fish market is smelly, lively and frenetic – watch where you step. Brightly painted boats bob along the shore while huge cases of everything from small sardines to fearsome langoustines are hawked. The action is fast and furious. (Jimbaran Beach; ⊙6am-3pm)

Morning Market   MARKET

3   ⊙ Map p62, C3

This is one of the best markets in Bali for a visit because a) it's compact so you can see a lot without wandering forever; b) local chefs swear by the quality of the fruit and vegetables – ever seen a cabbage that big?; and c) vendors are used to tourists trudging about. (Jl Ulu Watu; ⏱6am-noon)

Eating

Jimbaran Bay Seafood
SEAFOOD $$

4 Map p62, C1

The menu assures patrons that seeing the prices means 'Don't be worry!' Part of the rather staid northern group of warung, JBS is especially welcoming with a huge variety of tables: inside under cover, on the concrete terrace or out where your toes can tickle the sand. (JBS; 📞0361-701517; Jl Pantai Kedonganan; mains from 100,000Rp; ⏱11am-10pm)

⊙ Local Life
Ceramics Showcase

Modern warehouse **Jenggala Keramik Bali Ceramics** (Map p62, C5; 📞0361-703311; www.jenggala.com; Jl Ulu Watu II; ⏱8am-8pm) showcases beautiful ceramic homewares that are a favourite Balinese purchase. There's a viewing area where you can watch production, as well as a cafe. Ceramic courses are available for adults and children; a paint-a-pot scheme lets you create your own work of art (ready five days later after a trip through the kiln).

Made Bagus Cafe
SEAFOOD $$

5 Map p62, B4

Tucked away at the north end of the southern group of warung; the staff serving their narrow patch of tables on the beach here radiate charm. Go for one of the mixed platters and ask for extra sauce, it's that good. (📞0361-701858; off Jl Bukit Permai; meals 80,000-200,000Rp; ⏱noon-10pm)

Drinking

Rock Bar
BAR

6 🚇 Map p62, A5

Star of a thousand glossy articles written about Bali, this bar perched 14m above the crashing Indian Ocean is very popular. In fact, at sunset the wait to ride the lift down to the bar can top one hour. There's a no-backpacks, no-singlets dress code. The food is Med-flavoured bar snacks. (📞0361-702222; www.ayanaresort.com/rockbarbali; Jl Karang Mas Sejahtera, Ayana Resort; ⏱4pm-1am; 📶)

Jimbaran Beach Club
CAFE

7 🚇 Map p62, A5

Just in case Jimbaran Bay wasn't alluring enough, this beach bar has a long pool bordering the sand. Rather upscale, you can rent a comfy lounger and umbrella, and enjoy ordering from a long drinks and food menu. (📞0361-709959; Jl Pantai Muaya; minimum spend 200,000Rp; ⏱8am-11pm; 📶)

Understand

Seafood in Jimbaran

Enormous fresh prawns marinated in lime and garlic and grilled over coconut husks. Tick. A hint of post-sunset pink on the horizon. Tick. Stars twinkling overhead. Tick. A comfy teak chair settling into the beach while your toes play in the sand. Tick. An ice-cold beer. Tick. A strolling band playing the macarena. OK, maybe not a tick. But beachside seafood grills such as **Warung Ramayana** (☑0361-702859; off Jl Pantai Jimbaran; mains from 80,000Rp; ⏱11am-10pm) are a don't-miss evening out in Jimbaran, with platters of seafood that arrived fresh that morning to the market just up the beach.

Jimbaran has three distinct groups of seafood restaurants that cook fresh barbecued seafood every evening (and lunch at many), drawing tourists from across the south; almost all take credit cards. The open-sided affairs are right by the beach and perfect for enjoying sea breezes and sunsets. Tables and chairs are set up on the sand almost to the water's edge. Arrive before sunset, so you can get a good table and enjoy the solar show over a couple of beers before you dine.

Fixed prices for seafood platters in a plethora of varieties have become common and allow you to avoid the sport of choosing your fish and then paying for it by weight on scales that cause locals to break out in laughter. However, should you go this route, be sure to agree on costs first. Generally, you can enjoy a seafood feast, sides and a couple of beers for less than US$20 per person. Lobster (from US$30) will bump that figure up considerably.

▶ The northern seafood restaurants run south from the fish market along Jl Kedonganan and Jl Pantai Jimbaran. Most of these places are restaurantlike, with tables inside and out on the raked sand. However, the area lacks the fun atmosphere of the two areas to the south.

▶ The middle seafood restaurants are in a compact and atmospheric group just south of Jl Pantai Jimbaran and Jl Pemelisan Agung. These are the simplest affairs, with old-fashioned thatched roofs and wide-open sides. The beach is a little less manicured, with the fishing boats resting up on the sand.

▶ The southern seafood restaurants are a compact and festive collection of about a dozen places at the south end of the beach.

Explore

Ulu Watu & Around

The surf breaks grouped along the west coast of the Bukit Peninsula are the stuff of legend, and draw board riders from across the world. Most visitors, however, are mere surfing poseurs and come for the idyllic little beaches at the base of the cliffs. And no visit is complete without a visit to Ulu Watu's monkey-filled temple.

The Region in a Day

☼ Rise early in the hope of scoring a few waves to yourself at **Ulu Watu** (p71) while other surfers are still sleeping off the night before.

☼ Paddle in for an afternoon of exploring the many nooks and crannies of the Bukit Peninsula. Little beaches such as **Balangan** (p69), **Bingin** (p69) and **Padang Padang** (p69) are great finds that are worth minor treks across bad roads and along steep cliffside trails and stairs. Settle back on a lounger, enjoy a cold drink from a simple cafe and watch surfers pull into barrels offshore.

☾ Little places to stay – from simple surfer dives to posh boutique hotels – are where overnighters vanish to after dark (nightlife is very limited). But everyone should make time for **Pura Luhur Ulu Watu** (p71) near sunset. The temple and its views are great and the **dance performance** (p75) is a must.

Top Experiences

Ulu Watu's Beaches (p68)

 Best of Bali

Getting There

You'll need your own wheels – whether taxi, hire car or motorbike – to explore the Bukit.

🚗 **Taxi** Taxis from the Kuta–Seminyak area to Ulu Watu will cost around 200,000Rp one way. If day tripping be sure to arrange for a return as taxis don't hang around. Ulu Watu temple is often on tour itineraries.

🚶 **Walk** The various beaches are isolated from each other, so getting from one to the next requires some effort.

Top Sights
Ulu Watu's Beaches

One of Bali's hotspots is the booming west coast of the Bukit Peninsula with its string-of-pearls beaches. Often hidden at the base of cliffs, these white-sand visions of sunny pleasure are some of the best on Bali. You may have to drive along a road that barely qualifies as such and clamber down a steep path, but the reward is always worth it. Lazing away an afternoon at one of these coves is an essential Bali experience.

Padang Padang

Balangan Beach

Balangan Beach is a real find. A long and low strand at the base of the cliffs is covered with palm trees and fronted by a ribbon of near-white sand, picturesquely dotted with white sun umbrellas. Surfer bars (some with bare-bones sleeping rooms), cafes in shacks and even slightly more permanent guesthouses precariously line the shore where buffed First World bods soak up rays amid Third World sanitation. Balangan Beach is 6.5km off the main Ulu Watu road via Cenggiling.

Bingin Beach

An ever-evolving scene, Bingin comprises several unconventionally stylish lodgings scattered across – and down – the cliffs and on the strip of white sand below. One of Bukit's classic surf breaks, it's also famous as a beach hang-out with spectacular views. A 1km lane turns off the paved road (look for the thicket of accommodation signs), which in turn branches off the main Ulu Watu road at the small village of Pecatu. After you pay an elderly resident for access, you get to the beach from a main parking area. Follow the steep steps and trail down.

Padang Padang

Small in size but not in perfection (or popularity), this little cove is near the main Ulu Watu road where a stream flows into the sea. Experienced surfers flock here for the tubes. Parking is easy and it is a short walk through a temple and down a well-paved trail. If you're feeling adventurous, a much-longer stretch of white sand begins on the west side of the river. Ask locals how to get there.

☑ Top Tips

▶ Most of the beaches have namesake surf breaks offshore. Non-surfers enjoy watching the action on the water.

▶ Low-key cafes and vendors can be found on every beach.

▶ Although lacking sand, the cliffs at the Ulu Watu surf break have cafes with terraces, sun loungers and killer views.

▶ If you don't have your own transport (this is prime motorbike territory), arrange with your taxi or driver for pickup at the end of the day.

✕ Take a Break

Inside the shady bamboo **Nasa Café** (meals from 30,000Rp; ⊙8am-11pm), built on stilts above the sand, the wraparound view through the drooping thatched roof is of a vibrant azure ribbon of crashing surf. The simple Indo meals set the tone for the four very basic rooms (about 200,000Rp) off the bar. It's one of several similar choices.

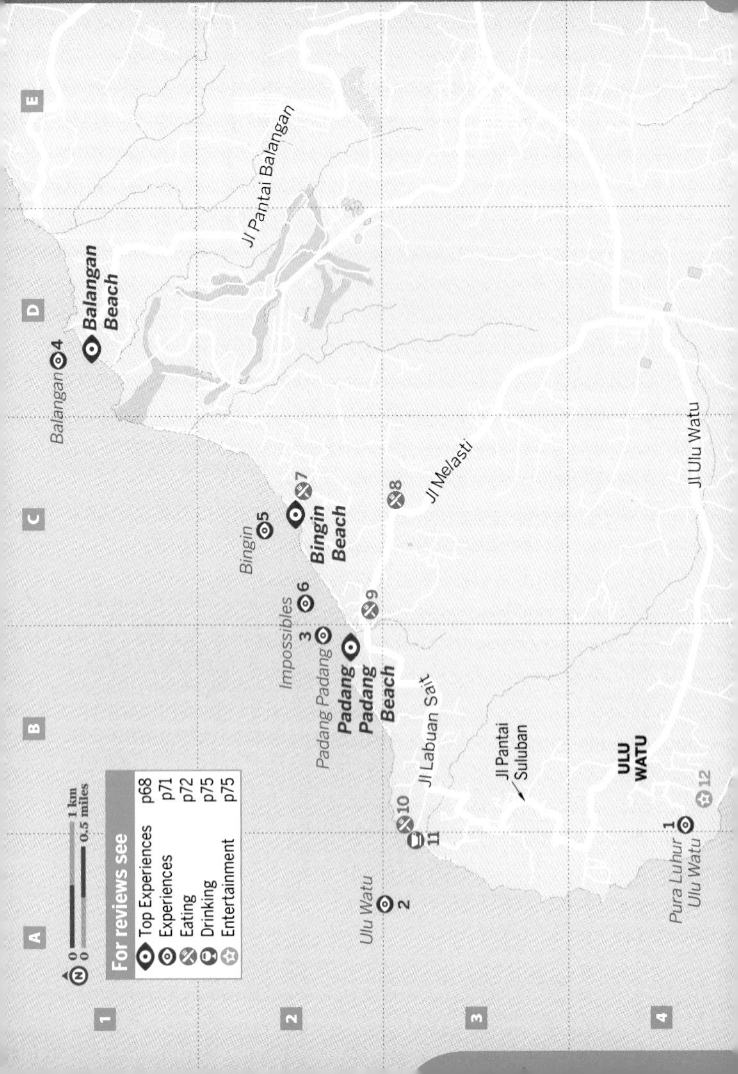

Balangan Beach

Jl Pantai Balangan

Balangan ◉4

Jl Melasti

Bingin ◉5

×7
◉
Bingin Beach

×8

Impossibles
3 ◉6

×9

Padang Padang ◉
Padang Padang Beach

Jl Labuan Sait

Jl Pantai Suluban

ULU WATU

✪12

Jl Ulu Watu

Jl Ulu Watu

For reviews see

◆ Top Experiences	p68
◉ Experiences	p71
✕ Eating	p72
◐ Drinking	p75
✪ Entertainment	p75

Ulu Watu ◉2

◉10
11

Pura Luhur ◉1
Ulu Watu

N
0   1 km
0   0.5 miles

MASTER / GETTY IMAGES ©

Pura Luhur Ulu Watu

Experiences

Pura Luhur
Ulu Watu
HINDU TEMPLE

 Map p70, B4

This important temple is perched
precipitously on the southwestern tip
of the peninsula, atop sheer cliffs that
drop straight into the ceaseless surf.
You enter through an unusual arched
gateway flanked by statues of Ganesha. Inside, the walls of coral bricks
are covered with intricate carvings
of Bali's mythological menagerie. (off
Jl Ulu Watu; adult/child 30,000/20,000Rp,
parking 2000Rp; ⊗8am-7pm)

Ulu Watu
SURFING

 Map p70, A3

On its day Ulu Watu is Bali's biggest
and most powerful wave. It's the
stuff of dreams and nightmares, and
definitely not one for beginners! Since

☑ Top Tip

Damn Monkeys

Pura Luhur Ulu Watu is home to
scores of grey monkeys. Greedy
little buggers, when they're not
energetically fornicating, they
snatch sunglasses, handbags, hats
and anything else within reach. If
you want to start a riot, peel them
a banana…

the early 1970s when it featured in the legendary surf flick *Morning of the Earth,* Ulu Watu has drawn surfers from around the world for left breaks that seem to go on forever.

Padang Padang

SURFING

3 Map p70, B2

This super-shallow, left-hand reef break off the very popular beach of the same name is just below some rickety accommodation joints where you can crash and watch the breaks. Check carefully before venturing out. It's a very demanding break that only works if it's over about 6ft from mid- to high tide.

STHAPORN KAMLANGHAN / SHUTTERSTOCK ©

Monkeys at Pura Luhur Ulu Watu (p71)

Balangan

SURFING

4 Map p70, D1

Off the long strip of sand that is Balangan Beach, the namesake surf break is a fast left over a shallow reef, unsurfable at low tide and good at midtide with anything over a 4ft swell; with an 8ft swell, this is one of the classic waves.

Bingin

SURFING

5 Map p70, C2

Given the walk down to Bingin Beach from the isolated parking area, you could be forgiven if you decide to leave your board up top, but don't. Waves here are best at midtide with a 6ft swell, when short but perfect left-hand barrels are formed, and you'll do well to have somebody on shore recording your action.

Impossibles

SURFING

6 Map p70, C2

Just north of Padang Padang, this challenging outside reef break has three shifting peaks with fast left-hand tube sections that can join up if the conditions are perfect.

Eating

Cashew Tree

CAFE $

7 Map p70, C2

The place to hang out in Bingin. Surfers and beachgoers gather in this large garden for tasty vegetarian

Understand

Bali's History

There are few traces of Stone Age people in Bali, although it's certain that the island was populated very early in prehistoric times. By the 9th century AD Bali had a society based on growing rice with the help of a complex irrigation system, probably very like that employed now; the Balinese had also begun to develop their rich cultural and artistic traditions. Hinduism followed hot on the heels of wider cultural development, and as Islam swept through neighbouring Java in the following centuries, the kings and courtiers of the embattled Hindu Majapahit kingdom began crossing the straits into Bali, making their final exodus in 1478. The priest Nirartha brought many of the complexities of the Balinese Hindu religion to the island.

Europeans Arrive

The first Europeans to set foot in Bali were Dutch seamen in 1597. At that time, Balinese prosperity and artistic activity, at least among the royalty, was at a peak. By the 18th century, bickering among various Balinese princes caused the island's power structure to fragment. In 1846 the Dutch landed military forces in northern Bali. Focus turned to the south and in 1906 Dutch warships appeared at Sanur. The Dutch forces landed despite Balinese opposition and had complete control of the island by 1908. Many thousands of Balinese – including royalty and priests – chose suicide in battle rather than occupation. Although under Dutch control and part of the Dutch East Indies, there was little development in Bali, and the common people noticed little difference between Dutch and royal rule.

Freedom

The Japanese occupied Bali in 1942 and conditions during WWII were grim. In August 1945, just days after the Japanese surrender, Sukarno, a prominent nationalist, proclaimed Indonesia's independence. Battles raged in Bali and elsewhere until the Dutch gave up and recognised Indonesia's independence in 1949. A prominent freedom fighter was Gusti Ngurah Rai, namesake of Bali's airport. The tourism boom, which started in the early 1970s, has brought enormous changes for better and worse. However, Bali's unique culture has proved to be remarkably resilient even as visitor numbers top three million per year.

Pura Luhur Ulu Watu's Significance

Pura Luhur Ulu Watu is one of several important temples to the spirits of the sea along the south coast of Bali. In the 11th century the Javanese priest Empu Kuturan first established a temple here. The complex was added to by Nirartha, another Javanese priest who is known for the seafront temples at Tanah Lot, Rambut Siwi and Pura Sakenan. Nirartha retreated to Ulu Watu for his final days when he attained *moksa* (freedom from earthly desires).

meals. Expect the likes of burritos, salads, sandwiches and smoothies. It's also a good spot for a drink; Thursday nights especially go off, attracting folk from up and down the coast with live bands. (☑0813 5321 8157; www.facebook.com/the-cashew-tree; Jl Pantai Bingan; meals from 40,000Rp; ⊙8am-10pm; 🛜🖈)

Drifter
CAFE $

8 Map p70, C3

Right at the turn to Bingin, this new outlet of the awesome Seminyak surf shop has a great cafe that will tempt anyone driving past. All the Drifter surf goods are on offer, plus you can settle back at a table inside or out for some of the Bukit's best coffee and a range of snacks, healthy lunches and alluring cakes. (http://driftersurf.com; Jl Labuan Sait; mains from 50,000Rp; ⊙10am-10pm)

Mango Tree Cafe
CAFE $$

9 Map p70, C2

This two-level cafe has a long menu of healthy options, including sandwiches, tasty burgers and fresh salads, soups and breakfast burritos. There are good juices and a decent drinks list. Try for a table under the namesake tree. The owner, Maria, is a generous delight. (☑0813 5309 8748; Jl Labuan Sait 17; mains 50,000-120,000Rp; ⊙7am-10pm)

Single Fin
CAFE $$

10 Map p70, B3

The views of the surf action from this triple-level cafe are breathtaking. Watch the never-ending swells march in across the Indian Ocean from this cliff-side perch; it's a great spot to watch surfers carving it up when the waves are big. Drinks here aren't cheap (or very good) and the food is merely passable, but come sunset, who cares?

Its Sunday session is a big event, when all the beautiful people arrive in full force for a night out. In peak season book a table. (☑0361-769941; www.singlefinbali.com; Jl Mamo; mains 65,000-150,000Rp; ⊙8am-11pm; 🛜)

WIDODO RUSLI / GETTY IMAGES ©

Kecak dance at Pura Luhur Ulu Watu

Drinking

Delpi
CAFE

11 Map p70, A3

A relaxed cafe-bar sitting on a cliff away from other cafe spots, with stunning views. One area is perched on a gigantic mushroom of concrete atop a rock out above the surf. The food is basic. (7am-8pm; 📶)

Entertainment

Kecak Dance
DANCE

12 Map p70, B4

Although the performance obviously caters for tourists, the gorgeous setting at Pura Luhur Ulu Watu in a small amphitheatre in a leafy part of the grounds makes it one of the more evocative on the island. The views out to sea are as inspiring as the dance. It's very popular in high season, expect crowds. (Pura Luhur Ulu Watu, off Jl Ulu Watu; 100,000Rp; sunset)

Explore

Nusa Dua & Tanjung Benoa

Popular with holidaymakers who love large resorts, Nusa Dua could be anywhere. It's a vast and manicured place where you leave the rest of the island behind as you pass the guards. Just to the north, slightly tatty Tanjung Benoa, lined with family-friendly, mostly midrange resort hotels, has a beach resort vibe without the artificial gloss.

The Region in a Day

☀ Mornings are active: start with a market visit as part of the Bumbu Bali Cooking School. Get wet and silly at one of Tanjung Benoa's many water-sports centres, such as **Benoa Marine Recreation** (p81). Straddle a banana boat and let the good times flow.

☀ Relax into the afternoon with a languid stroll on the **beach promenade** (p79) or hit the waves at **Nusa Dua** (p79). Peruse beautiful Balinese art in the shady **Pasifika Museum** (p79) or lose yourself at a spa; every resort has an upscale one and you can enjoy the lauded touch of the local edition of Seminyak's **Jari Menari** (p79).

☾ At night, consider skipping the many resort restaurants in favour of dining on the fabulous Balinese fare at **Bumbu Bali** (p80). Afterwards you might return to the beach promenade for a moonlit stroll with the heavenly light twinkling on the calm inshore waters.

 Best of Bali

Eating
Bumbu Bali (p80)

For Kids
Benoa Marine Recreation (p81)

Museums & Galleries
Pasifika Museum (p79)

Getting There

🚗 **Taxi** Taxis from the airport will cost about 150,000Rp to 175,000Rp, as will taxis to/from Seminyak. Note that the main road to the rest of Bali can get bogged down in traffic.

🚶 **Walk** A fine beach promenade runs much of the length of Nusa Dua and Tanjung Benoa. Otherwise, wide pavements abound in the former while the latter offers pedestrian peril along Jl Pratama.

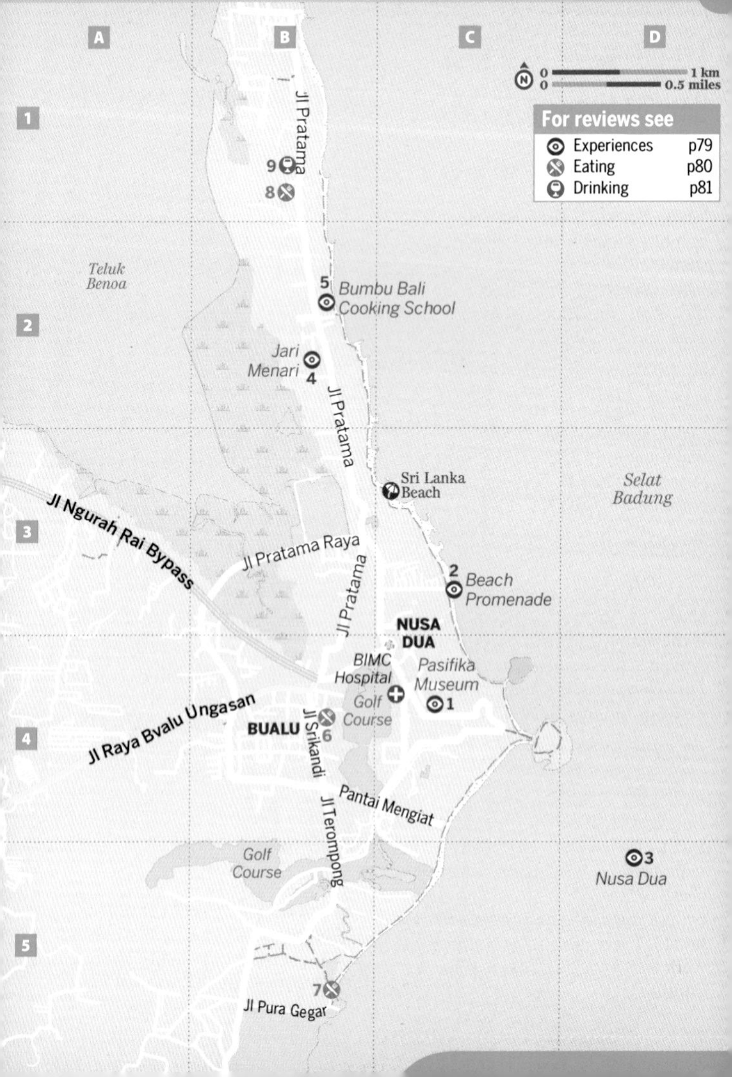
A
B
C
D
1
2
3
4
5
0 1 km
0 0.5 miles
For reviews see
Experiences p79
Eating p80
Drinking p81
Jl Pratama
9
8
Teluk Benoa
5 Bumbu Bali Cooking School
Jari Menari 4
Jl Pratama
Sri Lanka Beach
Selat Badung
Jl Ngurah Rai Bypass
Jl Pratama Raya
Jl Pratama
2 Beach Promenade
NUSA DUA
BIMC Hospital
Pasifika Museum
1
Golf Course
Jl Raya Bvalu Ungasan
BUALU
Jl Srikandi
6
Pantai Mengiat
Jl Terompong
Golf Course
3 Nusa Dua
7
Jl Pura Gegar

Experiences

Pasifika Museum   MUSEUM

1 Map p78, C4

When groups from nearby resorts aren't around, you'll probably have this large museum to yourself. A collection of art from Pacific Ocean cultures spans several centuries and includes more than 600 paintings (don't miss the tikis). The influential wave of European artists who thrived in Bali in the early 20th century is well represented. Look for works by Arie Smit, Adrien-Jean Le Mayeur de Merpres and Theo Meier. There are also works by Matisse and Gauguin. (☑0361-774559; www. museum-pasifika.com; Bali Collection shopping centre, block P; 70,000Rp; ☻10am-6pm)

Beach Promenade   WALKING

2 ◎ Map p78, C3

One of the nicest features of Nusa Dua is the 5km-long beach promenade that stretches the length of the resort from Pura Gegar in the south and north through Tanjung Benoa.

Nusa Dua   SURFING

3 ◎ Map p78, D5

During wet season, the reef off Nusa Dua has very consistent swells. The main break is 1km off the beach to the south of Nusa Dua – off Gegar Beach (where you can get a boat out to the break). There are lefts and rights that work well on a small swell at low to midtide.

Dishes at Bumbu Bali (p80)

Jari Menari   SPA

4 ◎ Map p78, B2

This branch of the famed Seminyak original offers all the same exquisite massages by the expert all-male staff. Call for transport. (☑0361-778084; www. jarimenarinusadua.com; Jl Pratama; massage from 385,000Rp; ☻9am-9pm)

Bumbu Bali Cooking School   COOKING

5 ◎ Map p78, B2

This much-lauded cooking school at the eponymous restaurant strives to get to the roots of Balinese cooking. Courses start with a 6am visit to

Local Life

Benoa's Places of Worship

The village of Benoa is a fascinating little fishing settlement that makes for a good stroll. Amble the narrow lanes of the peninsula's tip for a multicultural feast. Within 100m of each other are a brightly coloured **Chinese Buddhist temple**, a domed **mosque** and a **Hindu temple** with a nicely carved triple entrance. Enjoy views of the busy channel to the port. On the dark side, Benoa's backstreets hide Bali's illegal trade in turtles, although police raids are helping to limit it.

Jimbaran's fish and morning markets, continues in the large kitchen and finishes with lunch. (📞0361-774502; www.balifoods.com; Jl Pratama; course without/with market visit US$105/118; ⏰6am-3pm Mon, Wed & Fri)

Eating

Bumbu Bali   BALINESE $$

Long-time resident and cookbook author Heinz von Holzen, his wife Puji, and their well-trained and enthusiastic staff serve exquisitely flavoured dishes at this superb restaurant (see 5 Map p78, B2). Many diners opt for one of several lavish set menus. (📞0361-774502; www.balifoods.com; Jl Pratama; mains from 100,000Rp, set menus from 295,000Rp; ⏰noon-9pm)

Warung Dobiel   BALINESE $

6 ⊗ Map p78, B4

A bit of authentic food action amid the bland streets of Nusa, this is a good stop for *babi guling*. Pork soup is the perfect taste-bud awakener, while the jackfruit is redolent with spices. Diners perch on stools and share tables; service can be slow and tours may mob the place. Watch out for 'foreigner' pricing. (📞0361-771633; Jl Srikandi 9; meals from 40,000Rp; ⏰10am-3pm)

Nusa Dua Beach Grill   INTERNATIONAL $$

7 ⊗ Map p78, B5

A good spot for day trippers, this warm-hued cafe (hidden by the Mulia resort) is just south of Gegar Beach. The drinks menu is long, the seafood fresh and the relaxed beachy vibe intoxicating. (📞0851 0043 4779; Jl Pura Gegar; mains from 80,000Rp; ⏰8am-10.30pm)

Bali Cardamon   ASIAN $$

8 ⊗ Map p78, B1

A cut above most of the other restaurants on the Jl Pratama strip, this ambitious spot has a creative kitchen that takes influences from across Asia. It has some excellent dishes including pork belly seasoned with star anise. Sit under the frangipani trees or in the dining room. (📞0361-773745; www.balicardamon.com; Jl Pratama 97; mains 55,000-120,000Rp; ⏰8am-10pm)

Understand
Water Sports in Tanjung Benoa

Water-sports centres along Jl Pratama offer daytime diving, cruises, windsurfing and waterskiing. Each morning convoys of buses arrive with day trippers from all over south Bali, and by 10am parasailers float over the water.

All feature unctuous salespeople whose job it is to sell you the banana-boat ride of your dreams while you sit glassy-eyed in a thatched-roof sales centre and cafe. Check equipment and credentials before you sign up, as a few tourists have died in accidents.

Among the established water-sports operators is **Benoa Marine Recreation** (BMR; 🕿 0361-772438; www.bmrbali.com; Jl Pratama; ⊙8am-4pm). As if by magic, all operators have similar prices. Note that 'official' price lists are just the starting point for bargaining. Activities here include the following (with average prices):

Banana-boat rides Wild rides for two as you try to maintain your grasp on the inflatable fruit moving over the waves (US$20 per 15 minutes).

Glass-bottomed boat trips The non-wet way to see the denizens of the shallows (US$50 per hour).

Jet-skiing Go fast and belch smoke (US$25 per 15 minutes).

Parasailing Iconic; you float above the water while being towed by a speedboat (US$20 per 15-minute trip).

Snorkelling Trips include equipment and a boat ride to a reef (US$35 per hour).

One nice way to use the beach here is at **Tao** (🕿 0361-772902; www.taobali.com; Jl Pratama 96; mains 60,000-100,000Rp; ⊙8am-10pm; 🛜) restaurant, where for the price of a drink you can enjoy resort-quality loungers and a pool.

Drinking

Atlichnaya Bar

BAR

 Map p78, B1

The lively and convivial alternative to the stiff hotel bars, this rollicking place serves a long list of cheap mixed drinks and even offers massages (from 50,000Rp). There are cheap and cheery Indo and Western menu items as well. (🕿 0813 3818 9675; www.atlichnaya.com; Jl Pratama 88; ⊙8am-late; 🛜)

Explore

Sanur

The first Western artists to settle in Bali did so around Sanur more than 100 years ago. It's easy to see why: there's a long family-friendly beach protected by reefs, plenty of shady palm trees overhead and cool breezes off the ocean. Sanur isn't a party town, so visitors looking for serenity will be suitably chilled out here.

The Region in a Day

☀ Take advantage of the eastern light to hit **Sanur Beach** (p85) in the morning. Watch people fishing in traditional ways and try some water fun with **Surya Water Sports** (p86). Or get serious and get your scuba certification at **Crystal Divers** (p86).

☀ Enjoy a leisurely lunch with views over the water to Nusa Lembongan and Nusa Penida. **Warung Pantai Indah** (p87) and **Warung Mak Beng** (p87) are locally flavoured options. Once past noon, the shadows of the palm trees lengthen on the beach, so it's a good time for some spa action at **Jamu Wellness** (p86). Or just hit the shops. Jl Tamblingan has many choices including **A-Krea** (p89) for Bali-designed goods and **Ganesha Bookshop** (p89) for a perfect poolside read.

☾ For dinner, Jl Tamblingan again offers many choices. Try something Indonesian at **Pregina Warung** (p88) or go with Asian flair at **Three Monkeys Cafe** (p87). At the latter you can hear live jazz some nights. Finish off your evening with a stroll on the **beachfront walk** (p87), which ideally will offer moonlit views over the water.

 Best of Bali

Beaches
Sanur Beach (p85)

Pampering
Jamu Wellness (p86)

Power of Now Oasis (p86)

Diving & Snorkelling
Crystal Divers (p86)

Surya Water Sports (p86)

For Kids
Sanur Beach (p85)

Surya Water Sports (p86)

Bali Kite Festival (p86)

Getting There

🚗 **Taxi** Taxis from the airport will cost about 110,000Rp.

🚶 **Walk** You can easily walk the length of Sanur on the lovely beachfront walk. The main spine, Jl Tamblingan, is also easily walkable.

🚌 **Shuttle Bus** The Kura-Kura tourist bus (www.kura2bus.com) has a route linking Sanur with its Kuta hub. Buses run every two hours and cost 40,000Rp.

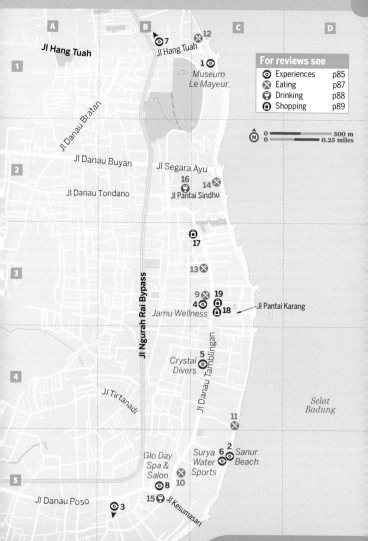

JI Hang Tuah

A

B 7

12

C

D

JI Hang Tuah

1

Museum
Le Mayeur

JI Danau Bratan

1

For reviews see

⊙ Experiences	p85
✕ Eating	p87
⊖ Drinking	p88
⊕ Shopping	p89

N 0 ——————— 500 m
    0 ——————— 0.25 miles

JI Danau Buyan

JI Segara Ayu

2

16

14

JI Danau Tondano

JI Pantai Sindhu

17

13

3

9 19

4

18

JI Pantai Karang

Jamu Wellness

JI Ngurah Rai Bypass

JI Danau Tamblingan

Crystal
Divers 5

4

JI Tirtanadi

Selat
Badung

11

Surya 6 2 Sanur
Water   Beach
Sports

Glo Day
Spa &
Salon

8

10

5

15 JI Kesumasari

JI Danau Poso 3

Sanur Beach

Experiences

Museum Le Mayeur
MUSEUM

1 ⊙ Map p84, C1

Artist Adrien-Jean Le Mayeur de Merpres (1880–1958) arrived in Bali in 1932, and married the beautiful Legong dancer Ni Polok three years later, when she was just 15. They lived in this compound back when Sanur was still a quiet fishing village. After the artist's death, Ni Polok lived in the house until she died in 1985. Despite security (some of Le Mayeur's paintings have sold for US$150,000) and conservation problems, almost 90 of Le Mayeur's paintings are displayed.

(☎0361-286201; Jl Hang Tuah; adult/child 20,000/10,000Rp; ⊙8am-3.30pm Sat-Thu, 8.30am-12.30pm Fri)

Sanur Beach
BEACH

2 ⊙ Map p84, C5

Sanur Beach curves in a southwesterly direction and stretches for more than 5km. It is mostly clean and overall quite serene – much like the town itself. Offshore reefs mean that the surf is reduced to tiny waves lapping the shore. With a couple of unfortunate exceptions, the resorts along the sand are low-key, leaving the beach uncrowded.

Power of Now Oasis
YOGA

3 ⊙ Map p84, B5

Enjoy a yoga class in this atmospheric bamboo pavilion looking out to Sanur Beach. Several levels are offered. Sunrise yoga is a popular choice. (📱0813 3831 5032; www.powerofnowoasis. com; Beachfront Walk, Hotel Mercure; classes from 100,000Rp)

Jamu Wellness
SPA

4 ⊙ Map p84, C3

This gracious spa has classy new digs and offers a range of treatments including a popular Earth and Flower Body Mask and a Kemiri Nut Scrub. (📱0811 389 9930; www.jamutraditionalspa.

 Top Tip

Kites over Sanur

You hear them overhead: huge kites 10m or more in length, with tails stretching another 100m and sporting noise-makers producing eerie humming and buzzing noises.

Each July, hundreds of Balinese and international teams descend – as it were – on open spaces north of Sanur for the **Bali Kite Festival**. They compete for an array of honours in categories such as original design and flight endurance. The action is centred around **Pantai Padang Galak**, about 1km up the coast from Sanur. You can catch kite-flying Balinese-style here from May to September.

com; Jl Danau Tamblingan 140; 1hr massage 350,000Rp; ⊙9am-9pm)

Crystal Divers
DIVING

5 ⊙ Map p84, C4

This slick diving operation has its own hotel (the Santai) and a large diving pool. Recommended for beginners, the shop offers a long list of courses, including PADI open-water (US$500). (📱0361-286737; www.crystal-divers.com; Jl Danau Tamblingan 168; dives from US$65)

Surya Water Sports
WATER SPORTS

6 ⊙ Map p84, C5

One of several water-sports operations along the beach, Surya is the largest. You can go parasailing (US$25 per ride), snorkelling by boat (US$50, two hours) or rent a kayak and paddle the smooth waters (US$15 per hour). (📱0361-287956; www.balisuryadivecenter. com; Jl Duyung 10; ⊙9am-5pm; 🚼)

Bali Orchid Garden
GARDENS

7 ⊙ Map p84, B1

Orchids thrive in Bali's warm weather and rich volcanic soil. At this garden you can see thousands of the flowers in a variety of settings. It's 3km north of Sanur along Jl Ngurah Rai, just past the major intersection with the coast road, and is an easy stop on the way to Ubud. (📱0361-701988; www. baliorchidgardens.com; Coast Rd; 100,000Rp; ⊙8am-6pm)

Glo Day Spa & Salon   SPA

8 Map p84, B5

An insider pick by the many local Sanur expats, Glo eschews a fancy setting for a clean-lined storefront. Services and treatments run the gamut, from skin and nail care to massages and spa therapies. (☏0361-282826; www.glo-day-spa.com; Jl Danau Poso 57, Gopa Town Centre; massage 1hr from 195,000Rp; ☺8am-6pm)

Eating

Three Monkeys Cafe   ASIAN $$

9 Map p84, C3

This branch of the splendid Ubud original is no mere knock-off. Spread over two floors, there's cool jazz playing in the background and live performances some nights. Set well back from the road, you can enjoy excellent coffee drinks on sofas or chairs. The creative menu mixes Western fare with pan-Asian creations. (☏0361-286002; www.threemonkeyscafebali.com; Jl Danau Tamblingan; meals 58,000-105,000Rp; ☺11am-11pm; 🛜)

Char Ming   ASIAN $$

10 Map p84, B5

Asian fusion with a French accent. A daily menu board lists the fresh seafood available for grilling. Look for regional dishes, many with modern flair. The highly stylised location features lush plantings and carved-wood

Local Life
Sanur's Beachfront Walk
Sanur's **beachfront walk** was the first in Bali and has been delighting locals and visitors alike from day one. More than 4km long, it curves past resorts, beachfront cafes, wooden fishing boats under repair and quite a few elegant old villas built decades ago by the wealthy expats who fell under Bali's spell. While you stroll, look out across the water to Nusa Penida.

details from vintage Javanese and Balinese structures. (☏0361-288029; www.charming-bali.com; Jl Danau Tamblingan N97; meals 60,000-250,000Rp; ☺5-11pm)

Warung Pantai Indah   CAFE $$

11 Map p84, C4

Sit at battered tables and chairs with your toes in the sand at this timeless beach cafe. It specialises in fresh barbecue-grilled seafood and cheap local dishes. (Beachfront Walk; mains 30,000-110,000Rp; ☺9am-9pm)

Warung Mak Beng   BALINESE $

12 Map p84, C1

You don't need a menu at this local favourite: all you can order is its legendary barbecued fish (*ikan laut goreng*), which comes with various sides and some tasty soup. Service is quick, the air fragrant and diners of all stripes very happy. (☏0361-282633; Jl Hang Tuah 45; meals 35,000Rp; ☺8am-9pm)

Pregina Warung BALINESE $$

13 ✗ Map p84, C3

Classic Balinese duck dishes and crowd-pleasers such as *sate* are mainstays of the interesting menu here. It serves local foods several cuts above the all-too-common bland tourist versions (try anything with duck). The dining room has spare, stylish wooden decor and features vintage photos of Bali. (✐0361-283353; Jl Danau Tamblingan 106; mains 40,000-80,000Rp; ⊘11am-11pm)

Byrdhouse
Beach Club INTERNATIONAL $$

14 ✗ Map p84, C2

With loungers, a swimming pool, a restaurant, bar and table tennis on-site, you could happily spend an entire day here by the beach. Check the club's Facebook page for upcoming events, including outdoor-cinema screenings and street-food stalls. (✐0361-288407; www.facebook.com/ byrdhousebeachclubbali; Segara Village, Sanur Beach; mains from 60,000Rp; ⊘6am-midnight; 🛜)

Drinking

Fire Station PUB

15 🍺 Map p84, B5

There's some old Hollywood style here at this open-fronted pub. Vaguely 1960s Hollywood-esque portraits line walls; you expect to see a young Dennis Hopper lurking in the rear. Enjoy pitchers of sangria and other interesting drinks along with a varied menu of good pub food that features many

---

Understand
Samur's Rulers & Artists

Sanur was one of the places favoured by Westerners during their pre-WWII discovery of Bali. Artists Miguel Covarrubias, Adrien-Jean Le Mayeur de Merpres and Walter Spies, anthropologist Jane Belo and choreographer Katharane Mershon all spent time here. The first tourist bungalows appeared in Sanur in the 1940s and '50s, and retiring expats followed. During this period Sanur was ruled by insightful priests and scholars, who recognised both the opportunities and the threats presented by expanding tourism. They established village cooperatives that owned land and ran tourist businesses, ensuring that a good share of the economic benefits remained in the community.

The priestly influence remains strong, and Sanur is one of the few communities still ruled by members of the Brahmana caste. It is known as a home of sorcerers and healers, and a centre for both black and white magic. The black-and-white chequered cloth known as *kain poleng*, which symbolises the balance of good and evil, is emblematic of Sanur.

the large, shady garden. The Mexican-style food features homegrown chilli peppers. (Borneo Bob's; ☎0361-289291; Jl Pantai Sindhu 11; mains from 40,000Rp; ⏱7.30am-11pm)

Shopping

Ganesha Bookshop
BOOKS

17 📍 Map p84, C3

A branch of Bali's best bookshop for serious readers. (www.ganeshabooksbali.com; Jl Danau Tamblingan 42; ⏱8am-9pm)

A-Krea
CLOTHING

18 📍 Map p84, C3

An excellent spot for souvenirs, A-Krea has a range of items designed and made in Bali in its attractive store. Clothes, accessories, homewares and more are all handmade. (☎0361-286101; Jl Danau Tamblingan 51; ⏱9am-9pm)

Goddess on the Go
CLOTHING

19 📍 Map p84, C3

Supercomfortable clothes for women who, like the name says, travel a lot. Many of the items are made with organic fibres. (☎0361-270174; www.goddessonthego.net; Jl Danau Tamblingan; ⏱9am-8pm)

PETER PTSCHELINZEW / GETTY IMAGES ©

Sculpture in Museum Le Mayeur gardens (p85)

specials. Order the fine Belgian beer, Duvel. (☎0361-285675; Jl Danau Poso 108; mains from 80,000Rp; ⏱4pm-late)

Kalimantan
BAR

16 🚇 Map p84, B2

This veteran boozer has an old *South Pacific* thatched charm and is one of several casual bars on this street. Enjoy cheap drinks under the palms in

Top Sights
Nusa Lembongan

Getting There

⚓ Boat Public fast boats from Sanur run three times a day and cost 150,000Rp one way (40 minutes). Fast tourist boats include those run by **Scoot** (www.scootcruise.com; one way adult/child 400,000/280,000Rp).

Alluring when seen from Sanur and east Bali, Nusa Lembongan is one of three islands that together comprise the Nusa Penida archipelago. It's the Bali many imagine but never find: rooms right on the beach, cheap beers with incredible sunsets, days spent surfing and diving, and nights spent engrossed in a new book or hanging with new friends. You can savour this bliss in a day or two away from the bright lights of south Bali.

Don't Miss

Jungutbatu Beach
Jungutbatu beach, a lovely arc of white sand with clear blue water, has views across to Gunung Agung in Bali. The village itself is pleasant, with quiet lanes, no cars and a couple of temples.

Mushroom Bay
Beautiful Tanjung Sanghyang, unofficially named Mushroom Bay after the mushroom corals offshore, has a crescent of bright white beach. The most interesting way to get here from Jungutbatu is to walk along the trail that starts from the southern end of the main beach and follows the coastline for a kilometre or so.

Diving & Snorkelling
There are great diving possibilities around the islands, from shallow and sheltered reefs to very demanding drift dives. The best dive sites include **Blue Corner** and **Jackfish Point** off Nusa Lembongan. **World Diving** (☑0812 390 0686; www.world-diving.com; Jungutbatu Beach; introductory dive 940,000Rp, openwater course 5,500,000Rp), based at Pondok Baruna, is very well regarded. It offers a complete range of courses, plus diving trips to dive sites all around the three islands. Good snorkelling can be had just off **Mushroom Bay** (**Tanjung Sanghyang**) and the **Bounty Pontoon**, as well as in areas off the north coast of the island.

Surfing
Surfing here is best in the dry season (April to September), when the winds come from the southeast. It's definitely not for beginners, and can be dangerous even for experts. There are three main breaks on the reef, all aptly named. From north to south are **Shipwrecks**, **Lacerations** and **Playgrounds**.

☑ Top Tips

▶ There are lots of simple guesthouses and a few small upmarket hotels.

▶ You can charter a boat from 150,000Rp per hour for snorkelling and for getting out to some surf breaks.

▶ You can easily walk to most places; bicycles cost 30,000Rp per day.

▶ There's no reliable ATM.

▶ A walk around much of the island is an all-day adventure.

✗ Take a Break

There are numerous beach cafes with all the usual standards plus fabulous views. For a cut above, **Indiana Kenanga** (☑0828 9708 4367; www.indiana-kenanga-villas.com; Jungutbatu Beach; r US$150-650; ❄ 🛜 ⛱) looks like it's been plucked from a glossy magazine and has an all-day menu of seafood and various surprises cooked up by the skilled chef.

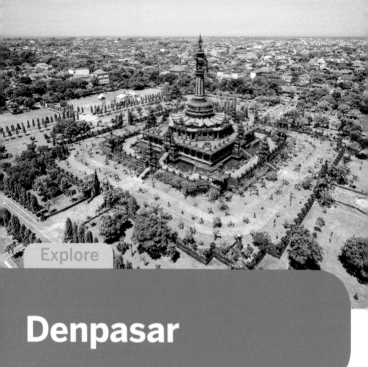

Explore

Denpasar

Bali's capital, home to most of the island's people and covering much of south Bali, shouldn't be overlooked by visitors. Here, chaotic and confusing streets mix with wide parks and boulevards that have a certain grandeur. Denpasar also boasts the island's main museums and largest markets, as well as a range of excellent restaurants.

The Region in a Day

 Visit the markets, **Pasar Badung** (p97) and **Pasar Kumbasari** (p97), in the morning when selection is greatest. The fruits and vegetables still look fresh and the flowers used for offerings are at their colourful best.

Lunch at any of the many local eateries, such as **Nasi Uduk Kebon Kacang** (p97) or **Depot Cak Asmo** (p96), which have excellent local dishes cooked to the standards demanded by the choosy Balinese. After, absorb Bali's history and culture at the comprehensive **Museum Negeri Propinsi Bali** (p95), the important temple **Pura Jagatnatha** (p96) and the surprisingly entertaining **Bajra Sandhi Monument** (p95; pictured left).

For visitors, Denpasar is an easy day trip from across south Bali and Ubud. However, it offers few reasons to linger after late afternoon.

 Best of Bali

Eating

Pasar Badung (p97)

Men Gabrug (p97)

Shopping

Pasar Badung (p97)

Museums & Galleries

Museum Negeri Propinsi Bali (p95)

Getting There

🚌 **Bus** Denpasar is a hub of public transport in Bali – you'll find buses and minibuses bound for all corners of the island.

🚶 **Walk** You can easily walk between the main markets and Museum Negeri Propinsi Bali. Most restaurants are located in Renon, a long walk from the markets or a 15,000Rp taxi ride.

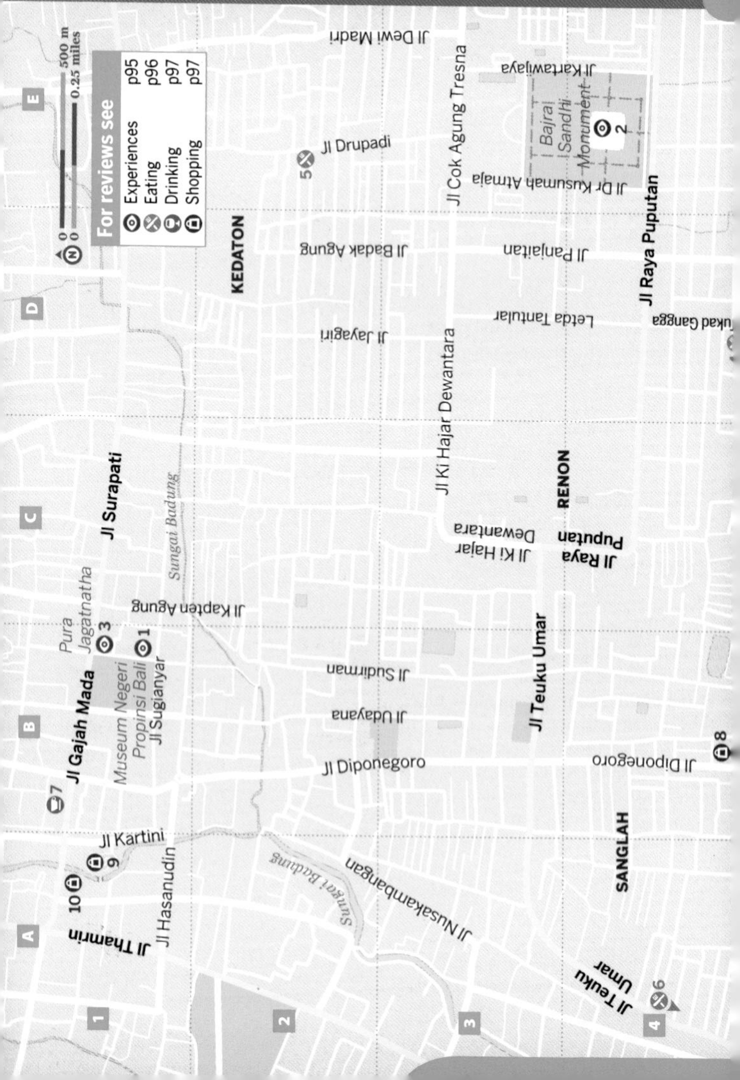
For reviews see
Experiences p95
Eating p96
Drinking p97
Shopping p97
0 500 m
0 0.25 miles
A
B
C
D
E
1
2
3
4
KEDATON
RENON
SANGLAH
Jl Dewi Madri
Jl Kartawijaya
Jl Cok Agung Tresna
Bajra Sandhi Monument
2
Jl Drupadi
5
Jl Dr Kusumah Atmaja
Jl Badak Agung
Jl Panjaitan
Jl Raya Puputan
Letda Tantular
Tukad Gangga
Jl Jayagiri
Jl Ki Hajar Dewantara
Jl Surapati
Sungai Badung
Jl Ki Hajar Dewantara
Jl Raya Puputan
Pura Jagatnatha
3
Jl Kapten Agung
1
Jl Teuku Umar
Jl Sudirman
Museum Negeri Propinsi Bali
Jl Gajah Mada
Jl Sugianyar
Jl Udayana
Jl Diponegoro
Jl Diponegoro
8
7
Jl Kartini
9
10
Jl Hasanudin
Jl Thamrin
Sungai Badung
Jl Nusakambangan
Jl Teuku Umar
6

Pura Jagatnatha (p96)

Experiences

Museum Negeri Propinsi Bali

MUSEUM

 Map p94, B1

Think of this as the British Museum or the Smithsonian of Balinese culture. It's all here, but unlike those world-class institutions, you have to work at sorting it out – the museum could use a dose of curatorial energy (and some new light bulbs). Most displays are labelled in English. The museum comprises several buildings and pavilions, including many examples of Balinese architecture, housing prehistoric pieces, traditional artefacts, Barong (a mythical lion-dog creature), ceremonial objects and rich displays of textiles. (☏0361-222680; adult/child 20,000/10,000Rp; ☉8am-4pm Sat-Thu, 8.30am-12.30pm Fri)

Bajra Sandhi Monument

MONUMENT

 Map p94, E4

The centrepiece to a popular park, this huge monument is as big as its name. Inside the vaguely Borobudur-like structure are dioramas tracing Bali's history. Note that in the portrayal of the 1906 battle with the Dutch, the King of Badung is literally a sitting target. Take the spiral stairs to the top for 360-degree views. (Monument to the Struggle of the People of Bali; ☏0361-264517; Jl Raya Puputan, Renon; adult/child 20,000/10,000Rp; ☉9am-6pm)

Understand
Responsible Travel

- -

To visit Bali responsibly, try to tread lightly as you go, with respect for both the land and the diverse cultures of its people.

Watch your use of water Water demand outstrips supply in much of Indonesia – even at seemingly green places like Bali. Take your hotel up on its offer to save water by not washing your sheets and towels every day.

Don't hit the bottle Those bottles of Aqua (a top local brand of bottled water, owned by Danone) are convenient but they add up. Since tap water is unsafe, ask your hotel if you can refill from their huge containers of drinking water. Some enlightened businesses already offer this service.

Support environmentally aware businesses The number of businesses committed to good environmental practices is growing fast.

Conserve power Turn off lights and air-con when not using them.

Bag the bags Refuse plastic bags, and say no to plastic straws too.

Leave the animals be Reconsider swimming with captive dolphins, riding elephants and patronising attractions where wild animals are made to perform for crowds, interactions that have been identified by animal welfare experts as harmful to the animals. And don't try to pet, feed or otherwise interact with animals in the wild as it disrupts their natural behaviour and can make them sick.

Pura Jagatnatha   HINDU TEMPLE

 Map p94, B1

The state temple, built in 1953, is dedicated to the supreme god, Sanghyang Widi. Part of its significance is its statement of monotheism. Although the Balinese recognise many gods, the belief in one supreme god (who can have many manifestations) brings Balinese Hinduism into conformity with the first principle of Pancasila – the 'Belief in One God'. (Jl Surapati; admission free)

Eating

Depot Cak Asmo   INDONESIAN $

 Map p94, D4

Join the government workers and students from the nearby university for superb dishes cooked to order in the bustling kitchen. Order the buttery and crispy *cumi cumi* (calamari) battered in *telor asin* (a heavenly mixture of eggs and garlic). Fruity ice drinks are a cooling treat. An English-language menu makes ordering a breeze. It's halal, so there's no alcohol. (☑ 0361-798 9388; Jl Tukad Gangga; mains from 15,000Rp; ☺ 9.30am-10.30pm)

Men Gabrug
BALINESE $

 5 Map p94, E2

A favourite sweet treat for Balinese of all ages is *jaje laklak* – disks of rice flour cooked in an open-air cast-iron pan, and redolent of coconut. One of the best places to get them is at this family-run outlet where the cooking takes place right on the street. (Jl Drupadi; snacks from 10,000Rp; ☺ 8am-6pm)

Nasi Uduk Kebon Kacang
INDONESIAN $

 6 Map p94, A4

Open to the street, this spotless cafe serves up Javanese treats such as *nasi uduk* (sweetly scented coconut rice with fresh peanut sauce) and *lalapan* (a simple salad of fresh lemon-basil leaves). Chicken dishes win raves. (☑ 0812 466 6828; Jl Teuku Umar 230; meals 12,000-25,000Rp; ☺ 8am-midnight)

Drinking

Bhineka Djaja
COFFEE

 7 Map p94, B1

Home to Bali's Coffee Co, this storefront sells locally grown beans and makes a mean espresso, which you can enjoy at the two tiny tables while watching the bustle of Denpasar's old main drag. (☑ 0361-224016; Jl Gajah Mada 80; coffee 7000Rp; ☺ 9am-4pm Mon-Sat)

Shopping

Jepun Bali
TEXTILES

 8 Map p94, B4

It's like your own private version of the Museum Negeri Propinsi Bali: Gusti Ayu Made Mardiani is locally famous for her *endek* (used for traditional sarongs) and *songket* (silver- or gold-threaded) clothes woven using traditional techniques. You can visit her gracious home and workshop and see the old machines in action, then ponder her beautiful polychromatic selections in silk and cotton. She's in south Denpasar. (☑ 0361-726526; Jl Raya Sesetan, Gang Ikan Mas 11; ☺ call for appointment)

Pasar Badung
MARKET

 9 Map p94, A1

Bali's largest food market is recovering from a 2016 fire. While rebuilding continues, there are ad hoc stalls in the surrounding area. Busy in the mornings and evenings, it's a great place to browse and bargain. You'll find produce and food from all over the island, and will revel in the range of fruit and spices on offer. (Jl Gajah Mada; ☺ 6am-5pm)

Pasar Kumbasari
MARKET

10 Map p94, A1

Handicrafts, a plethora of vibrant fabrics and costumes decorated with gold are just some of the goods at this huge market across the river from Pasar Badung. Note that the malls have taken their toll and there are a lot of empty stalls. (Jl Gajah Mada; ☺ 8am-6pm)

Explore

Ubud

When you think about what really sets Bali apart from other beachy destinations, it is the culture, the rice fields and the inherent charm of the people – qualities that Ubud has in spades. Bali's rich artistic and dance traditions are here to enjoy. And there are plenty of sybaritic spas and splendid restaurants to keep things from getting too high-minded.

The Region in a Day

☀ Get up with the sun and walk through Ubud's rice fields. Afterwards try to think up new words for 'green' and 'beautiful' as you enjoy a coffee at one of Ubud's many great cafes, such as **Freak Coffee** (p112) or **Coffee Studio Seniman** (p113). Now might be a good time for some shopping at the boutiques on Jl Dewi Sita.

☼ Have a healthy lunch at **Moksa** (p111), or go completely local at **Warung Teges** (p111). Then enjoy some pampering: consider yoga at **Yoga Barn** (p103), a range of therapies at **Taksu Spa** (p108) or a luxurious massage at **Ubud Sari Health Resort** (p102).

☾ No night is complete without a taste of Ubud's famed dance culture. Choose your dance performance and enjoy traditions that are the very soul of the Balinese. After, savour dinner at **Locavore** (p103), **Mozaic** (p112), **Pica** (p111) or another fine spot. Ubud goes to bed early: after a glimpse of the moonlight on the rice fields, enjoy a great night's sleep in the cool mountain air; or extend your evening with some Western tunes at the **Laughing Buddha** (p113).

For a local's day in Ubud, see p102.

Top Experiences

Touring Ubud's Rice Fields (p100)

 Local Life

A Perfect Ubud Day (p102)

 Best of Bali

Pampering

Yoga Barn (p103)

Taksu Spa (p108)

Ubud Sari Health Resort (p102)

Eating

Locavore (p103)

Mozaic (p112)

Pica (p111)

Nasi Ayam Kedewatan (p112)

Warung Teges (p111)

Getting There

🚗 **Taxi** Taxis with the cartel from the airport to Ubud cost 300,000Rp. A hired car with driver to the airport will cost about the same.

🚶 **Walk** Ubud is all about walking, although ubiquitous local guys offer 'transport' for about 20,000Rp to 40,000Rp depending on distance.

Top Sights
Touring Ubud's Rice Fields

There's nothing like a walk through the verdant rice fields of Ubud to make things all right with the world. These unbelievably green and ancient terraces spill down lush hillsides to rushing rivers below. As you wander along, you can hear the symphony of frogs, bugs and the constant gurgle of water coursing through channels. Most fields produce three crops a year and even on a short walk you'll see tender shoots, vibrant seas of green and the grain-heavy heads of mature plants.

Walk It Yourself
From the Ibah Luxury Villas driveway in Campuan, take the path to the left, where a walkway crosses the river to the small and serene Pura Gunung Lebah. Follow the concrete path north onto the ridge between the two rivers where you can see the rice fields above Ubud folding over the hills in all directions.

Bali Bird Walks
For keen birdwatchers, this popular **tour** (☎0361-975009; www.balibirdwalk.com; Jl Raya Campuan; tour incl lunch US$37; ⏱9am-12.30pm Tue, Fri, Sat & Sun), started by Victor Mason, draws flocks. A gentle morning's walk will give you the opportunity to see maybe 30 of the 100 or so local species. The tours leave from the former Beggar's Bush Bar on Jl Raya Campuan.

Herb Walks
Three-hour **walks** (☎0812 381 6024; www.baliherbalwalk.com; walks per person 200,000Rp; ⏱8.30am) through lush Bali landscape; medicinal and cooking herbs and plants are identified and explained in their natural environment. Includes herbal drinks.

Banyan Tree Cycling
Day-long **tours** (☎0813 3879 8516; www.banyantreebiketours.com; tours adult/child from US$55/35) of remote villages in the hills above Ubud. It's locally owned, and the tours emphasise interaction with villagers. These are very popular and have inspired a bevy of competitors.

Make a Discovery
Parts of Ubud may seem chock-a-block with development but you'd be surprised how often you can find beautiful emerald green rice fields, just by ducking down a lane. Try this along Jl Bisma or even Monkey Forest Rd.

☑ Top Tips
► Tail a family of local ducks through the rice fields; if a path peters out you can always go back.

► Bring water, a good hat, decent shoes and wet-weather gear for the afternoon showers.

► Try to start walks at daybreak, before it gets too hot.

► Some entrepreneurial rice farmers have erected little toll gates across their fields. You can detour around them or pay a fee (never, ever accede to more than 10,000Rp).

✕ Take a Break
A stroll through Ubud's beautiful rice fields calls for a snack. Bali Buda has an organic market and **bakery** (www.balibuda.com; Jl Raya Ubud; ⏱8am-8pm). where you can choose from a range of tasty treats to stash in your daypack (snacks from 10,000Rp). The blueberry muffins are especially good.

Local Life
A Perfect Ubud Day

Spas, shopping, cafes, markets, temples, dance and more can fill your Ubud days. Here's an ideal stroll combining a little of all that will work whether you are staying for a few days or are day tripping. This walk takes you through the heart of the town, and you'll find plenty of discoveries along the way.

....

❶ Cleanse Yourself Inside & Out

There are so many places in Ubud for health and spa treatments that you almost need therapy to sort through them. But an excellent place to start is **Ubud Sari Health Resort** (Map p104, D3; ☎0361-974393; www.ubudsari.com; Jl Kajeng 35; 1hr massage from 200,000Rp; ⏰9am-8pm), where function trumps form. The setting is pastoral and includes all manner of herbs and healing plants.

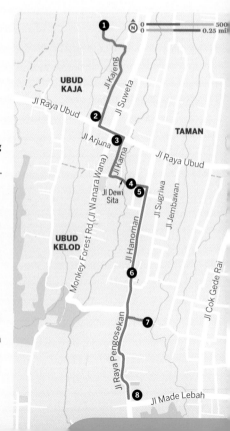

❷ Ubud's Water Temple

An oasis in the heart of Ubud, **Pura Taman Saraswati** (Map p104, C4; Jl Raya Ubud; admission free) is one of the town's most picturesque spots. Waters from the temple at the rear feed a pond overflowing with iconic lotus blossoms. There are usually a few wannabe artists trying to capture the moment. No matter how frenetic the traffic is outside, here you'll feel nothing but calm.

❸ Ubud's Hidden Produce Market

Hidden in the far southeast corner of the overcrowded and schlock-filled Ubud Market is this real, working **Produce Market** (Jl Raya Ubud; ☺6am-1pm). Get here early enough and you'll find Ubud's top chefs bargaining for their day's ingredients. Browse Bali's fab range of fresh foodstuffs and see how many types of fruit you *can't* identify.

❹ Dewi Sita Creations

The relatively short, curving and hilly Jl Dewi Sita is lined with some of Ubud's most creative shops. Everything from handmade paper to jewellery to luscious beauty products can be found at its little boutiques.

❺ Lunch at Locavore to Go

By now it's time for lunch. Although you need reservations months ahead to get a table for dinner at Dewi Sita's legendary **Locavore** (Map p104, D5; ☎0361-977733; www.restaurantlocavore.com; Jl Dewi Sita; 5-/7-course menu 675,000/775,000Rp; ☺noon-2pm & 6-10pm; P❄🛜), their simple storefront cafe, **Locavore to Go** (Map p104, D5; Jl Dewi Sita; mains 50,000-120,000Rp; ☺8.30am-6pm; 🛜), is easily accessed for lunch. This much simpler affair uses their famous charcuterie for tasty brunches.

❻ Shopping Jl Hanoman

Ubud has myriad art shops, clothing boutiques and galleries. Some of the most interesting are found along Jl Hanoman. Take your time wandering this long, slanting street and see what discoveries you make; many shops are owned by the designers of the goods within. Stop in one of the many little cafes for a break.

❼ Yoga Barn

It can seem like every other person in Ubud is either a yoga student or a yoga teacher. Even if you're not yet either, you can get in on the action at the iconic **Yoga Barn** (☎0361-971236; www.theyogabarn.com; off Jl Raya Pengosekan; classes from 130,000Rp; ☺7am-8pm), an ever-growing nexus of mellow.

❽ Dance Performance

Ubud has cultural performances virtually every night, and even if you are just visiting for a day, it's well worth staying for an evening performance before heading back to your hotel or villa in the south. One of the best venues is the **Arma Open Stage** (Map p104, D8; ☎0361-976659; Jl Raya Pengosekan), as it attracts some of the best troupes.

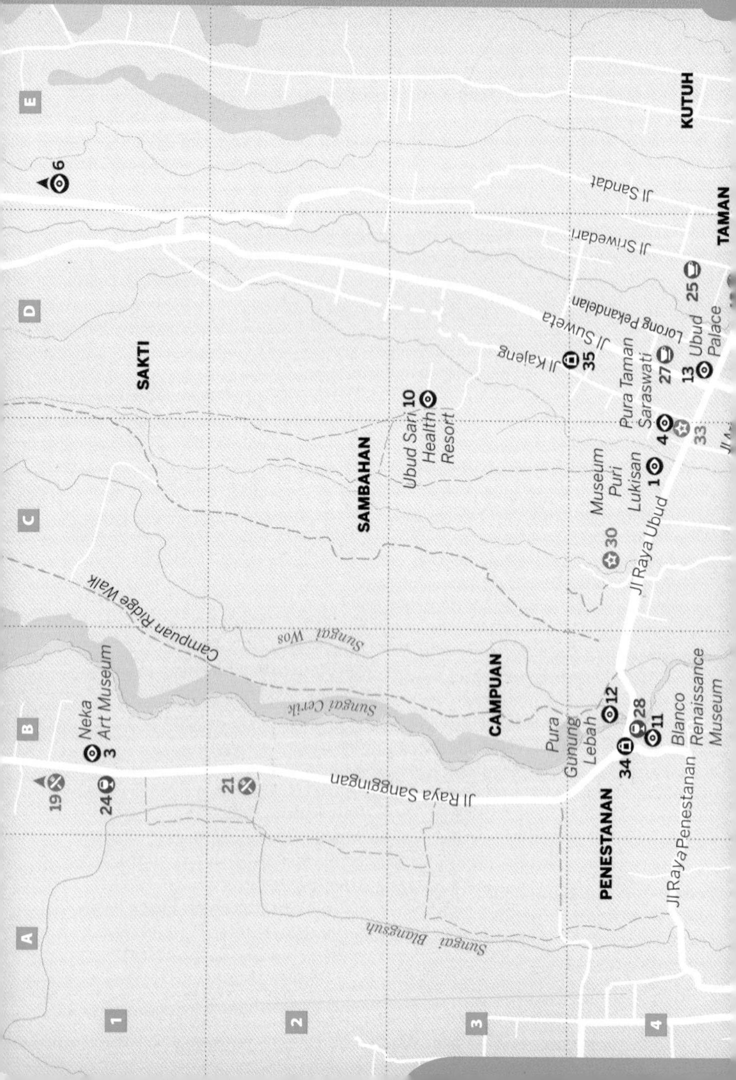

KUTUH

TAMAN

Jl Sandat

Jl Sriwedari

25

Lorong Pekandelan

13 Ubud
Palace

27

Pura Taman
Saraswati

Jl Suweta

Jl Kajeng

35

SAKTI

33

4

1

Museum
Puri
Lukisan

D

Ubud Sari 10
Health
Resort

SAMBAHAN

30

Jl Raya Ubud

C

Campuan Ridge Walk

Sungai Wos

Sungai Cerik

Neka
Art Museum
3

B

CAMPUAN

12

Pura
Gunung
Lebah

28

11

Blanco
Renaissance
Museum

19

24

34

21

Jl Raya Sanggingan

PENESTANAN

Jl Raya Penestanan

Sungai Blangsuh

A

E

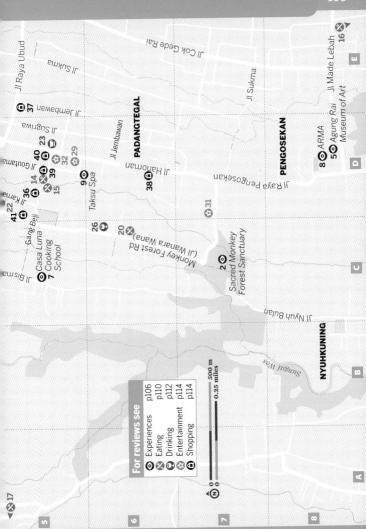

Jl Cok Gede Rai

16 ✕

Jl Made Lebah

Jl Raya Ubud

Jl Sukma

Jl Jembatan

37 🖾

Jl Sukma

PADANGTEGAL

Jl Sugriwa

23 🖾

40

32

29 💿

Jl Goutama

Jl Jembawan

Jl Hanoman

38 💿

PENGOSEKAN

ARMA

8 💿

Agung Rai   Jl Raya

5 💿   Museum of Art

14 🖾   39

36 ✕   15

22

41

Gang Beji

Taksu Spa

9 💿

Jl Raya Pengosekan

31 ✪

Casa Luna

7 💿 Cooking

School

26 💿

20 ✕ (Jl Wanara Wana)

Monkey Forest Rd

2 💿

Sacred Monkey

Forest Sanctuary

Jl Nyuh Bulan

NYUHKUNING

Jl Bisma

17 ✕

Sungai Wos

For reviews see

💿	Experiences	p106
✕💿✕	Eating	p110
💿💿	Drinking	p112
🎭	Entertainment	p114
🛍	Shopping	p114

500 m

0.25 miles

N

E

D

C

B

A

5

6

7

8

Experiences

Museum Puri Lukisan   MUSEUM

1 Map p104, C4

It was in Ubud that the modern Balinese art movement started, when artists first began to abandon purely religious themes and court subjects for scenes of everyday life. This museum displays fine examples of all schools of Balinese art, and all are well labelled in English. It was set up by Rudolf Bonnet, with Cokorda Gede Agung Sukawati (a prince of Ubud's royal family) and Walter Spies. (Museum of Fine Arts; ☏0361-975136; www.museumpurilukisan.com; off Jl Raya Ubud; adult/child 85,000Rp/free; ☺9am-5pm)

Sacred Monkey Forest Sanctuary   PARK

2 Map p104, C7

This cool and dense swathe of jungle, officially called Mandala Wisata Wanara Wana, houses three holy temples. The sanctuary is inhabited by a band of over 600 grey-haired and greedy long-tailed Balinese macaques who are nothing like the innocent-looking doe-eyed monkeys on the brochures. Nestled in the forest is the interesting **Pura Dalem Agung** temple. (Mandala Wisata Wanara Wana; ☏0361-971304; www.monkeyforestubud.com; Monkey Forest Rd; adult/child 40,000/30,000Rp; ☺8.30am-6pm)

Neka Art Museum   GALLERY

3 Map p104, B1

The creation of Suteja Neka, a private collector and dealer in Balinese art, Neka Art Museum has an excellent and diverse collection. It's a good place to learn about the development of painting in Bali. You can get an overview of the myriad local painting styles in the **Balinese Painting Hall**. Look for the *wayang* (puppet) works. (☏0361-975074; www.museumneka.com; Jl Raya Sanggingan; adult/child 50,000Rp/free; ☺9am-5pm Mon-Sat, noon-5pm Sun)

✓ Top Tip

Cycling Ubud

Many shops and hotels in central Ubud display mountain bikes for hire. The price is usually a negotiable 35,000Rp per day. If in doubt about where to rent, ask at your hotel and someone with a bike is soon likely to appear.

In general, the land is dissected by rivers running south, so any east–west route will involve a lot of ups and downs as you cross the river valleys. North–south routes run between the rivers, and are much easier going, but can have heavy traffic. Most of the sites in Ubud are reachable by bike.

Riding a bike is an excellent way to visit the many museums and cultural sites located around Ubud, although you'll need to consider your comfort level with traffic south of Ubud.

JOHN ELK III / GETTY IMAGES ©

Pura Taman Saraswati

Pura Taman Saraswati

HINDU TEMPLE

4  Map p104, C4

Waters from the temple at the rear of this site feed the pond in the front, which overflows with pretty lotus blossoms. There are carvings that honour Dewi Saraswati, the goddess of wisdom and the arts, who has clearly given her blessing to Ubud. There are regular dance performances by night. (Jl Raya Ubud; admission free)

Agung Rai Museum of Art

GALLERY

5  Map p104, D8

Founded by Agung Rai as a museum, gallery and cultural centre, the impressive ARMA is the only place in Bali to see haunting works by influential German artist Walter Spies, alongside many more masterpieces. The museum is housed in several traditional buildings set in gardens with water coursing through channels. The collection is well labelled in English. (ARMA; ☏0361-976659; www.armabali.com; Jl Raya Pengosekan; adult/child incl drink 60,000Rp/free; ☺9am-6pm, Balinese dancing 3-5pm Mon-Fri, classes 10am Sun)

Balinese Farm Cooking School

COOKING

6  Map p104, E1

Spend a day out in untrammelled countryside 18km north of Ubud *and* learn how to cook Balinese food. This highly recommended cooking course is held in a village of lush gardens and run by villagers who are passionate about organic farming. Students learn about local produce and foods, and it's all cleverly designed for tourists: herbs are grown in raised beds so there's no stooping etc. (✆0812 3953 4446; http://balinesecooking.net; Banjar Patas, Taro; 1-day course 400,000Rp)

Casa Luna Cooking School
COOKING

7 ◉ Map p104, C5

Regular cooking courses are offered at Honeymoon Guesthouse and/or **Casa Luna restaurant** (✆0361-977409; www.casalunabali.com; Jl Raya Ubud; meals from 50,000Rp; ⊙8am-10pm). Half-day courses cover ingredients, cooking techniques and the cultural background of the Balinese kitchen (note, not all courses include a visit to the market). Each day has a different focus so you can return for many days of instruction. Tours are also offered, including a good one to the Gianyar night market. (✆0361-973282; www.casalunabali.com; Honeymoon Guesthouse, Jl Bisma; classes from 450,000Rp)

ARMA
CULTURAL TOUR

8 ◉ Map p104, D8

A cultural powerhouse offering classes in painting, woodcarving, gamelan and batik. Other courses include Balinese history, Hinduism and architecture. (✆0361-976659; www.armabali.com; Jl Raya Pengosekan; classes from US$25; ⊙9am-6pm)

Taksu Spa
SPA

9 ◉ Map p104, D5

Taksu has a long and rather lavish menu of treatments, as well as a strong focus on yoga. There are private rooms for couples massages; a breezy, healthy cafe; and a range of classes. Very popular, Taksu is expanding to additional locations. (✆0361-479 2525; www.taksuspa.com; Jl Goutama; massage from 375,000Rp; ⊙9am-9pm)

Ubud Sari Health Resort
SPA

10 ◉ Map p104, D3

A spa and hotel in one. It is a serious place with extensive organic treatments bearing such names as 'total tissue cleansing'. Beside a long list of daytime spa and salon services, there are packages that include stays at the hotel. Many treatments focus on cleaning out your colon. (✆0361-974393; www.ubudsari.com; Jl Kajeng 35; 1hr massage from 200,000Rp; ⊙9am-8pm)

Blanco Renaissance Museum
MUSEUM

11 ◉ Map p104, B4

The picture of Antonio Blanco (1912–99) mugging with Michael Jackson says it all. His surreal palatial neo-Renaissance home and namesake museum captures the artist's theatrical spirit. Blanco came to Bali from Spain via the Philippines. Playing the role of an eccentric artist à la Dalí, he is known for his expressionist art and illustrated poetry that incorporates a mix of styles and mediums. Enjoy

Understand
Showing Respect

Bali has a well-deserved reputation for being mellow, which is all the more reason to respect your hosts, who are enormously forgiving of faux pas if you're making a sincere effort. Be aware and respectful of local sensibilities, and dress and act appropriately, especially in rural villages and at religious sites. When in doubt, let the words 'modest' and 'humble' guide you.

Dos & Don't

▶ You'll see shorts and short skirts everywhere on locals but overly revealing clothing is still frowned upon, as is wandering down the street shirtless quaffing a beer.

▶ Many women go topless on Bali's beaches, offending locals who are embarrassed by foreigners' gratuitous nudity.

▶ Don't touch anyone on the head; it's regarded as the abode of the soul and is therefore sacred.

▶ Do pass things with your right hand. Even better, use both hands. Just don't use only your left hand, as it's considered unclean.

▶ Beware of talking with hands on hips – a sign of contempt, anger or aggression (as displayed in traditional dance and opera).

▶ Beckon someone with the hand extended and using a downward waving motion. The Western method of beckoning is considered very rude.

▶ Don't make promises of gifts, books and photographs that are soon forgotten. Pity the poor local checking their mailbox or email inbox every day.

▶ Cover shoulders and knees if visiting a temple or mosque; in Bali, a *selandong* (traditional scarf) or sash plus a sarong is usually provided for a small donation or as part of the entrance fee.

▶ Women are asked not to enter temples if they're menstruating, pregnant or have recently given birth. At these times women are thought to be *sebel* (ritually unclean).

▶ Don't put yourself higher than a priest, particularly at festivals (eg by scaling a wall to take photos).

Understand

Spas, Yoga, Healers & More

Ubud brims with salons and spas where you can heal, pamper, rejuvenate or otherwise focus on your personal needs, physical and mental. Visiting a spa is at the top of many a traveller's itinerary and the business of spas, yoga and other treatments grows each year. Expect the latest trends from any of the many practitioners (the bulletin board outside Bali Buddha is bewildering) and prepare to try some new therapies, such as 'pawing'. If you have to ask, you don't want to know. You may also wish to seek out a *balian* (traditional healer).

Bali Spirit Festival (www.balispiritfestival.com; day pass US$150; ⊙Mar/early Apr) is a hugely popular yoga, dance and music festival from the people behind the Yoga Barn in Ubud. There are more than 100 workshops and concerts, plus a market and more. It's usually held in early April but may begin in late March.

the waterfall and exotic birds on the way in, and good views over the river. (☎0361-975502; www.blancomuseum.com; Jl Raya Campuan; adult/child 80,000Rp/free; ⊙9am-5pm)

Pura Gunung Lebah   HINDU TEMPLE

 12 Map p104, B4

This old temple, which sits on a jutting rock at the confluence of two tributaries of the Sungai Cerik (*campuan* means 'two rivers'), has recently benefitted from a huge building campaign. The setting is magical; listen to the rushing waters while admiring the impressive multistepped *meru* (multitiered shrine) and a wealth of ever-more elaborate carvings. (off Jl Raya Campuan)

Ubud Palace   PALACE

13 Map p104, D4

The palace and its temple, **Puri Saren Agung** (cnr Jl Raya Ubud & Jl Suweta; admis-

sion free), share a space in the heart of Ubud. The compound was mostly built after the 1917 earthquake and the local royal family still lives here. You can wander around most of the large compound and explore the many traditional, though not excessively ornate, buildings. (cnr Jl Raya Ubud & Jl Suweta; admission free; ⊙8am-7pm)

Eating

Locavore   FUSION $$$

14 Map p104, D5

The foodie haven in Ubud, this temple to locally sourced foods is the town's toughest table. Book weeks in advance. Meals are degustation and can top out at nine courses; expect the joy to last three hours. Chefs Eelke Plasmeijer and Ray Adriansyah in the open kitchen are magicians; enjoy the show (and go for the wine pairings). (☎0361-

977733; www.restaurantlocavore.com; Jl Dewi Sita; 5-/7-course menu 675,000/775,000Rp; ⊘noon-2pm & 6-10pm; P ✳ 🛜)

Pica
SOUTH AMERICAN $$$

15 Map p104, D5

Much-acclaimed, the South American cuisine here is one of Ubud's culinary highlights thanks to the young couple behind this excellent restaurant. From the open kitchen, dishes making creative use of beef, pork, fish, potatoes and more issue forth in a diner-pleasing stream. The house sourdough bread is superb. (📞0361-971660; Jl Dewi Sita; mains 160,000-300,000Rp; ⊘11am-10pm Tue-Sun)

Warung Teges
BALINESE $

16 Map p104, E8

The *nasi campur* (rice with a choice of side dishes) is better here than almost anywhere else around Ubud. The restaurant gets just about everything right, from the pork sausage to the chicken, the *babi guling* (suckling pig) and even the tempeh. The sambal is legendary: fresh, tangy, with a perfect amount of heat. (Jl Cok Rai Pudak; mains from 25,000Rp; ⊘8am-6pm)

Moksa
VEGETARIAN $$

17 Map p104, A5

Forget that farm-to-table stuff, at Moksa it's farm-to-fork-to-farm. Based at their own permaculture farm, the restaurant shows the extraordinary meals that can be made with vegetables prepared simply. Half the dishes are

raw, half cooked. The changing menu usually features the popular 'Lasagne Love', which includes nut cheese and pesto. The setting is rustic with polish amidst the farm. (📞0361-479 2479; www.moksaubud.com; Gang Damai, Sayan; mains 40,000-80,000Rp; ⊘10am-9pm Tue-Sun)

Hujon Locale
INDONESIAN $$

18 Map p104, D4

From the team of the critically acclaimed Mama San in Seminyak, Hujon Locale is one of Ubud's most enjoyable restaurants. The menu mixes traditional Indonesian dishes with modern, creative flair, from Achenese prawn curry to slow-braised Sumatran lamb curry. The setting

Market in Ubud

within a chic colonial-style two-storey bungalow is made for a balmy evening. Great cocktails. (📞0361-849 3092; www.hujanlocale.com; Jl Sriwedari 5; mains 110,000-200,000Rp; 🕐noon-10pm; 🛜)

Nasi Ayam Kedewatan   BALINESE $

19 🍴 Map p104, B1

Few locals making the trek up the hill through Sayan pass this Bali version of a roadhouse without stopping. The star is *sate lilit*: chicken is minced, combined with an array of spices including lemongrass, then moulded onto bamboo skewers and grilled. Stock up on traditional Balinese road snacks: fried chips combined with nuts and spices. (📞0361-742 7168; Jl Raya Kedewatan; meals from 25,000Rp; 🕐9am-6pm)

Three Monkeys   FUSION $$

20 🍴 Map p104, C6

Order a kaffir-lime mojito and settle back amid the frog symphony of the rice fields. Add the glow of tiki torches for a magical effect. By day there are sandwiches, salads and gelato. At night there's a fusion menu of Asian classics. (📞0361-975554; www.three monkeyscafebali.com; Monkey Forest Rd; mains 60,000-185,000Rp; 🕐8am-10pm; 🛜)

Mozaic   FUSION $$$

21 🍴 Map p104, B2

Chef Chris Salans oversees this much-lauded top-end restaurant. Fine French fusion cuisine features on a constantly changing seasonal menu that takes its influences from

tropical Asia. Dine in an elegant garden twinkling with romantic lights or an ornate pavilion. Choose from four tasting menus, one of which is a surprise. (📞0361-975768; www.mozaic-bali.com; Jl Raya Sanggingan; 6-course menu 700,000Rp; 🕐6-10pm; 🛜)

Gelato Secrets   GELATERIA $

22 🍴 Map p104, D5

This temple to frozen goodness has fresh flavours made from local fruits and spices, such as dragonfruit cinnamon or cashew black sesame. (www.gelatosecrets.com; Monkey Forest Rd; treats from 20,000Rp; 🕐10am-10.30pm)

Locavore to Go   CAFE $$

From the same team as critically acclaimed Locavore down the road, this much simpler affair uses their famous charcuterie for tasty brunches ranging from breakfast burgers and bahn mi to pulled-pork brioche all in an open-fronted cafe (see 32 ⭐ Map p104, D5). A mandatory Slow Food stop. (📞0361-977733; Jl Dewi Sita; mains 50,000-120,000Rp; 🕐8.30am-6pm; 🛜)

Drinking

Freak Coffee   COFFEE

23 🍴 Map p104, D5

The name is appropriate here as these people are coffee fanatics. The best Bali beans are hand-selected and then roasted with precision before being brewed with an attention to detail that would please a persnickety mad scientist.

Overlaying this is a quest to produce fantastic coffee with the lowest carbon footprint possible. Enjoy the results at this simple, open-fronted shop. (📞0361-898 7124; Jl Hanoman 1; ⊗8am-8pm)

Room 4 Dessert LOUNGE

24 Map p104, B1

Celebrity chef Will Goldfarb, who gained fame as *the* dessert chef in Manhattan, runs what could be a nightclub except that it just serves dessert. Get some friends and order the sampler. Pair everything with his line-up of classic and extraordinary cocktails and wines, then let the night pass by in a sugary glow. (📞0821 4429 3452; www.room4dessert.asia; Jl Raya Sanggingan; treats from 100,000Rp; ⊗6pm-late)

Coffee Studio Seniman CAFE

25 Map p104, D4

That 'coffee studio' moniker isn't for show; all the equipment is on display at this temple of single-origin coffee. Take a seat on the designer rocker chairs and choose from an array of pour-over, siphon, Aeropress or espresso coffees using a range of quality Indonesian beans. It's also popular for food (mains from 50,000Rp) and drinks in the evening. (📞0812 3607 6640; www.senimancoffee.com; Jl Sriwedari 5; coffee from 30,000Rp; ⊗8am-10pm; 🛜)

Laughing Buddha LOUNGE

26 Map p104, C6

People crowd the street at night in front of this small cafe with live music

 Top Tip

Refill Your Water Bottle

The number of plastic water bottles emptied in Bali's tropical heat daily and then tossed in the trash is colossal. In Ubud there are a few places where you can refill your water bottle (plastic or reusable) for a small fee, usually 3000Rp. The water is the same Aqua brand that is preferred locally and you'll be helping to preserve Bali's beauty, one plastic bottle at a time. A good central location is **Pondok Pekak Library & Learning Centre** (Map p104, D5; 📞0361-976194; www.pondok pekaklibrary.com; Monkey Forest Rd; classes per hr from 100,000Rp; ⊗9am-5pm Mon-Sat, 1-5pm Sun).

Monday through Saturday nights. Rock, blues, vocals, acoustic, jazz and more. The kitchen is open until 1am for Asian bites (mains 40,000Rp to 70,000Rp). (📞0361-970928; www.facebook.com/laughingbuddhabali; Monkey Forest Rd; ⊗9am-late; 🛜)

Rio Helmi Gallery & Cafe CAFE

27 Map p104, D4

As tasty as one of their famous cupcakes, this cafe in the eponymous gallery is the perfect place to pause for a coffee and/or an all-day breakfast and to soak up some Ubud vibe. Settle back with a fine beverage and take in Helmi's renowned photography. (📞0361-972304; http://riohelmi.com; Jl Suweta 5; mains from 60,000Rp; ⊗7am-7pm)

Bridges
LOUNGE

28 Map p104, B4

The namesake bridges are right outside this multilevel restaurant with sweeping views of the gorgeous river gorge. You'll hear the rush of the water over rocks far below while you indulge in a top-end cocktail *on* the rocks. There are gourmet bites for sharing and a long wine list for exploring. Popular happy-hour drink specials. (☑0361-970095; www.bridgesbali.com; Jl Raya Campuan; ⊙11am-11.30pm, happy hour 4-7pm)

Entertainment

Paradiso
CINEMA

29 ⭐ Map p104, D5

This organic vegetarian restaurant also screens two or three nightly movies at its surprisingly plush 150-seat cinema. The price of admission is redeemable against items from the Earth Cafe menu – so a great deal. During the day it hosts regular talks and events; check the website for schedule. (☑0361-783 5545; www.paradisoubud.com; Jl Gautama Selatan; 50,000Rp incl food or drinks; ⊙films from 5pm)

Pura Dalem Ubud
DANCE

30 ⭐ Map p104, C4

At the west end of Jl Raya Ubud, this open-air venue has a flame-lit carved-stone backdrop and is one of the most evocative places to see a dance performance. (Jl Raya Ubud)

Pondok Bamboo Music Shop
PUPPET THEATRE

31 ⭐ Map p104, D7

Short-attention-span-friendly shadow-puppet shows are performed here by noted experts. (☑0361-974807; Monkey Forest Rd; tickets 75,000Rp; ⊙performances 8pm Mon & Thu)

Padangtegal Kaja
DANCE

32 ⭐ Map p104, D5

A simple, open terrace in a convenient location. In many ways this location hints at what dance performances have looked like in Ubud for generations. (Jl Hanoman)

Pura Taman Saraswati
DANCE

33 ⭐ Map p104, C4

The beauty of the setting may distract you from the dancers, although at night you can't see the lily pads and lotus flowers that are such an attraction by day. (Ubud Water Palace; Jl Raya Ubud)

Arma Open Stage
DANCE

Has some of the best troupes performing Kecak and Legong dance (see **8** Map p104, D8). (☑0361-976659; Jl Raya Pengosekan)

Shopping

Rumble
CLOTHING

34 🔒 Map p104, B4

Owned by the drummer of the famous Balinese punk act Superman is Dead,

Understand

The Magic of Dance

Few travel experiences can be more magical than attending a Balinese dance performance, especially in Ubud. Cultural entertainment keeps people returning and sets Bali apart from other tropical destinations. Ubud is the perfect base for the nightly array of performances and for accessing events in surrounding villages. Dances performed for visitors are generally adapted and abbreviated to some extent to make them more enjoyable, but usually have appreciative locals in the audience (or peering around the screen!). It's also common to combine the features of more than one traditional dance in a single performance.

The website Ubud Now & Then (www.ubudnowandthen.com) has schedules of special events and performances. Also check with Ubud Tourist Information (p116), which has performance information and sells tickets (usually 75,000Rp to 125,000Rp). For performances outside Ubud, transport is often included in the price. Tickets are also sold at many hotels, at the venues and by street vendors – all charge the same price. Performances typically last about 1½ hours. One note about your phone: nobody wants to hear it; nor do the performers want your flash in their eyes.

The Best of the Dance Troupes

All dance groups on Ubud's stages are not created equal. Here are our top picks:

Semara Ratih High-energy, creative Legong interpretations. The best local troupe musically.

Gunung Sari Legong dance; one of Bali's oldest and most respected troupes.

Semara Madya Kecak dance; especially good for the hypnotic chants. A mystical experience for some.

Tirta Sari Legong and Barong dance.

Cudamani One of Bali's best gamelan troupes. They rehearse in Pengosekan.

Watch for frequent temple ceremonies. Go around 8pm and you'll see Balinese dance and music in its full cultural context. You'll need to be appropriately dressed – your hotel or a local can tell you what to do.

Rumble stocks a cool selection of locally designed streetwear. Fittingly, it's right at the entrance to the madcap Blanco Renaissance Museum (p108). (Rmbl; www.xrmblx.co; Jl Raya Campuan; ☺9am-10pm)

Threads of Life Indonesian Textile Arts Center
TEXTILES

35 Map p104, D4

This small, professional textile gallery and shop sponsors the production of naturally dyed, handmade ritual textiles from around Indonesia. It exists to help recover skills in danger of being lost to modern dyeing and weaving methods. Commissioned pieces are displayed in the gallery, which has good explanatory material. Also runs regular textile-appreciation courses (classes from 75,000Rp).

Top Tip

Tourist Information

Ubud Tourist Information (Map p104, D4; Fabulous Ubud; ☎0361-973285; www.fabulousubud.com; Jl Raya Ubud; ☺8am-8pm; 🛜) is run by the Ubud royal family and is the one really useful tourist office in Bali. It has a good range of information and a noticeboard listing current happenings and activities. The staff can answer most regional questions and it has up-to-date information on ceremonies and traditional dances held in the area; dance tickets and tours are sold here.

(☎0361-972187; www.threadsoflife.com; Jl Kajeng 24; ☺10am-7pm)

Kou
COSMETICS

36 Map p104, D5

The perfume of luxurious locally handmade organic soaps wafts as you enter. Put some in your undies drawer and it'll smell fine for weeks. The range is unlike that found in chain stores selling luxe soap. It also operates Kou Cuisine (p117). (☎0361-971905; Jl Dewi Sita; ☺9am-8pm)

Ganesha Bookshop
BOOKS

37 Map p104, E5

A quality bookshop with an excellent selection of titles on Indonesian studies, travel, arts, music, fiction (including used books) and maps. Great staff recommendations. (www.ganeshabooks bali.com; Jl Raya Ubud; ☺9am-8pm)

Ashitaba
HOMEWARES

38 Map p104, D6

Tenganan, the Aga village of east Bali, is where the beautiful rattan items sold here are produced. Containers, bowls, purses and more (from US$5) display the fine and intricate weaving. (☎0361-464922; Jl Hanoman; ☺10am-8pm)

CreArt Story
ARTS & CRAFTS

39 Map p104, D5

A shop for readers of *Adbusters*: a no-brand brand store. The store's ethos is selling goods that aren't

Performer at Ubud Palace (p110)

made by faceless poorly paid people. The handicrafts here are responsibly sourced and come with their own stories of their origin. (☎0813 3881 8829; www.facebook.com/creartstoryshop; Jl Goutama 20; ⏱11am-8pm)

Tn Parrot
CLOTHING

40 🔒 Map p104, D5

The trademark parrot of this T-shirt shop is a characterful bird and he (she?) appears in many guises on this shop's line of custom T-shirts. Designs range from cool to groovy to offbeat. Everything is made from high-quality cotton that's been preshrunk. (www.tnparrot.com; Jl Dewi Sita; ⏱10am-8pm)

Pondok Bamboo Music Shop
MUSICAL INSTRUMENTS

Hear the music of a thousand bamboo wind chimes at this store (see **31** 🔒 Map p104, D7) owned by noted gamelan musician Nyoman Warsa, who offers music lessons and stages shadow-puppet shows. (☎0361-974807; Monkey Forest Rd; ⏱10am-8pm)

Kou Cuisine
HOMEWARES

41 🔒 Map p104, D5

A repository of small and exquisite gifts, including beautiful little jars of jam made with Balinese fruit or containers of sea salt harvested from along Bali's shores. (☎0361-972319; Monkey Forest Rd; ⏱10am-8pm)

Explore

East Bali

Wandering the roads of east Bali is one of the island's great pleasures. Rice terraces spill down hillsides under swaying palms, wild volcanic beaches are washed by pounding surf and age-old villages soldier on with barely a trace of modernity. Padangbai is a port town with a real traveller vibe, while Semarapura has important relics from Bali's royal past.

The Region in a Day

☀ East Bali makes a splendid day trip from either south Bali or Ubud. Start your day watching for the towering Gunung Agung, the island's most sacred volcano. Clouds usually obscure it in the heat of the day. While it's still cool, drive the Sidemen Road and maybe stop for a rice-field ramble. Or enjoy a morning treat at **Uforia** (p123).

☀ For lunch, try one of the choices along the coast road such as local fave **Warung Ida** (p125) or an elegant lunch with a view at **Bali Asli** (p123). After lunch, take time at a beach such as **Pantai Lebih** (p121) or enjoy one of the many black-sand beaches towards Sanur. Wander historic Semarapura and **Kertha Gosa** (p122); check out the local markets.

☾ Day trippers will want to be back home by dark. But if you're staying, Padangbai has an alluringly mellow beach vibe. Otherwise, resorts and hotels great and small are scattered along the coast and near Sidemen.

 Best of Bali

Beaches
Pantai Klotek (p121)

Pasir Putih (p123)

Pantai Lebih (p121)

Diving & Snorkelling
Padangbai (p124)

Eating
Semarapura Market (p121)

Gianyar Night Market (p125)

Warung Ida (p125)

Getting There

🚗 **Car** From south Bali or Ubud you can arrange a car and driver for about US$60 per day to go touring in the east.

🚶 **Walk** Within Semarapura and Padangbai you can easily walk between sights. However, you'll need transport to get from one part to another of this large region.

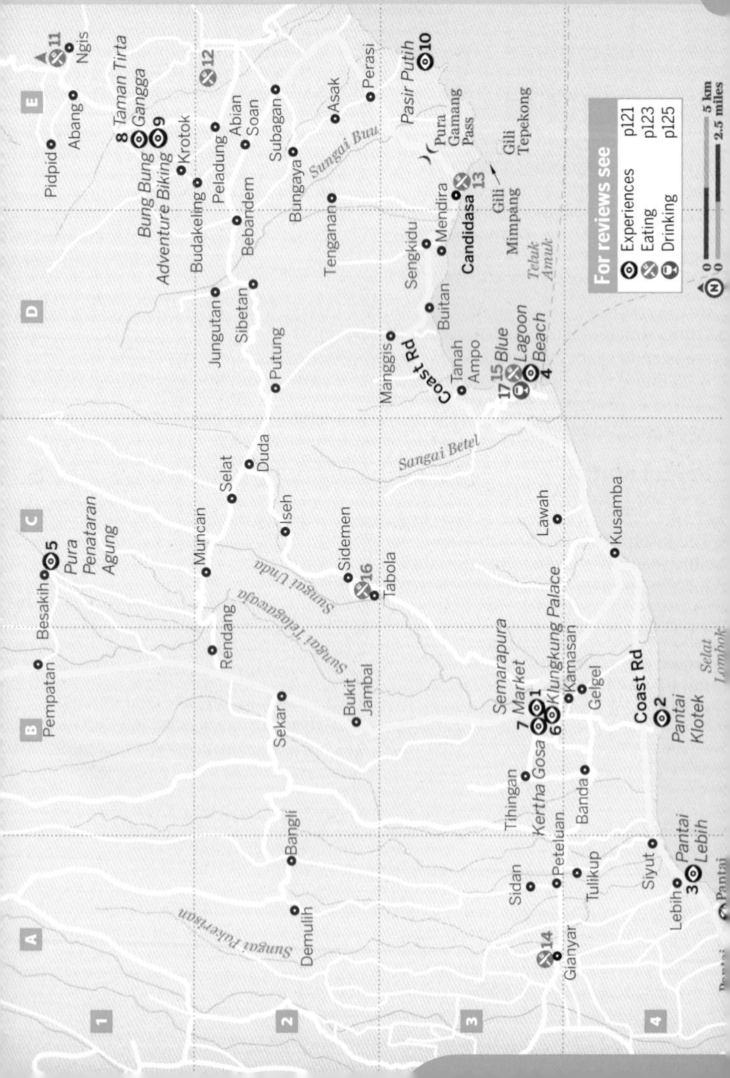

Ngis ▲11 ⊗

Abang ●

8 Taman Tirta Gangga

Pidpid ●

Bung Bung 9 ◉◉ ⊗12
Adventure Biking Krotok ●

Peladung ●

Budakeling ●

Bebandem ●

Abian ● Soan

Subagan ●

Asak ●

Perasi ●

Pasir Putih ⊗10

Pura Gamang Pass

Gili Tepekong

Jungutan ●

Sibetan ●

Bungaya ●

Tenganan ●

Sungai Buu

Sengkidu ●

Mendira ⊗13
Candidasa

Gili Mimpang

Putung ●

Buitan ●

Tanah Ampo

Teluk Amuk

Manggis ●

Coast Rd

15 Blue ⊗
17 ⊗ Lagoon 4
Beach

Besakih ● ◉5

Pura Penataran Agung

Muncan ●

Selat ●

Duda ●

Sangai Betel

Pempatan ●

Rendang ●

Iseh ●

Sidemen ●

Lawah ●

Kusamba ●

Sungai Telagawaja

Sungai Unda

Tabola ●

⊗16

Sekar ●

Bukit ● Jambal ●

Semarapura

Klungkung Palace

Kamasan ●

Selat Lombok

Bangli ●

Tihingan ●

7 Market ◉◉1
Kertha Gosa 6 ◉◉

Gelgel ●

Coast Rd

Pantai ◉2 Klotek

Sidan ●

Peteluan ●

Banda ●

Demulih ●

Tulikup ●

Siyut ●

Lebih ● Pantai Lebih

Sungai Pakerisan

Gianyar ●

⊗14

Pantai ◉3

For reviews see

◉ Experiences	p121
⊗ Eating	p123
▼ Drinking	p125

0 —————— 5 km
0 —————— 2.5 miles

N ⊕

A | B | C | D | E

1 | 2 | 3 | 4

Experiences

Semarapura Market   MARKET

1  Map p120, B3

Semarapura's sprawling market is a vibrant hub of commerce and a meeting place for people of the region. You can easily spend an hour wandering about the warren of stalls on three levels. It's grimy, yes, but also endlessly fascinating. Huge straw baskets of lemons, limes, tomatoes and other produce are islands of colour amid the chaos. A plethora of locally made snacks are offered in profusion; try several. (Jl Diponegoro; ⏱6am-5pm)

Pantai Klotek   BEACH

2 Map p120, B4

The lovely 800m drive along the hilly road off the coast road is but a prelude to this very interesting beach. The quiet at the temple, **Pura Watu Klotok**, belies its great significance: sacred statues are brought here from Pura Besakih temple for ritual cleansing. There are snack vendors and a new beachside brick walk. Admire the pale blue flowers – they're sacred – on the wild midori shrubs here.

Pantai Lebih   BEACH

3 Map p120, A4

Lebih Beach has glittering mica-infused sand. Just off the main road, the large Sungai Pakerisan (Pakerisan River), which starts near Tampaksir-

Statue at Klungkung Palace (p122)

ing, reaches the sea near here. Fishing boats line the shore, which is fitting as there's a strip of warungs with specialities that include *sate ikan laut* (fish satay) and rich seafood soup. The air is redolent with the smell of barbecued fish; this is an excellent stop for lunch. Large convenience stores offer supplies good for other beaches.

Blue Lagoon Beach   BEACH

4 Map p120, D3

On the far side of Padangbai's eastern headland, about a 500m walk, is the small, light-sand Blue Lagoon Beach, an idyllic place with a couple of cafes and gentle, family-friendly surf.

Local Life

Pura Dalem Sidan

When driving east from Gianyar you come to the turn-off to Bangli about 2km out of Peteluan. Follow this road for about 1km until you reach a sharp bend, where you'll find Sidan's **Pura Dalem Sidan**. This good example of a temple of the dead has very fine carvings. In particular, note the sculptures of Durga with children by the gate and the separate enclosure in one corner of the temple – this is dedicated to Merajapati, the guardian spirit of the dead.

Pura Penataran Agung
HINDU TEMPLE

5 Map p120, C1

Pura Penataran Agung, the most important temple in the Pura Basakih temple complex, is built on six levels, terraced up the slope, with the entrance approached from below, up a flight of steps. This entrance is an imposing *candi bentar* (split gateway) and, beyond it, the even more impressive *kori agung* is the gateway to the second courtyard. (admission per person 15,000Rp, plus per vehicle 5000Rp)

Klungkung Palace
HISTORIC BUILDING

6 Map p120, B3

When the Dewa Agung dynasty moved here in 1710, the Semara Pura was established. The palace was laid out as a large square, believed to be in the form of a mandala, with courtyards, gardens, pavilions and moats. Most of the original palace and grounds were destroyed by the 1908 Dutch attacks; the **Pemedal Agung**, the gateway on the south side of the square, is all that remains of the palace itself – check out its carvings. (Jl Puputan; adult/child 12,000/6000Rp; ⏰6am-6pm)

Kertha Gosa
HISTORIC BUILDING

7 Map p120, B3

In the northeastern corner of the Klungkung Palace complex, the Kertha Gosa was effectively the supreme court of the Klungkung kingdom, where disputes and cases that could not be settled at the village level were eventually brought. This open-sided pavilion is a superb example of Klungkung architecture. The ceiling is completely covered with fine paintings in the Klungkung style. These paintings, done on asbestos sheeting, were installed in the 1940s, replacing cloth paintings that had deteriorated. (Hall of Justice; Klungkung Palace)

Taman Tirta Gangga
PALACE

8 Map p120, E1

Amlapura's water-loving rajah, after completing his lost masterpiece at Ujung, had another go at building the water palace of his dreams in 1948. He succeeded at Taman Tirta Gangga, which has a stunning crescent of rice-terrace-lined hills for a backdrop. (adult/child 20,000/10,000Rp, parking 2000Rp; ⏰site 24hr, ticket office 7am-6pm)

Bung Bung Adventure Biking

CYCLING

9 ⊙ Map p120, E1

Ride downhill through the simply gorgeous rice fields, terraces and river valleys around Tirta Gangga with this grassroots tour company. Itineraries last from two to four hours and include use of a mountain bike and helmet, water and plenty of local encounters. The office is at **Homestay Rijasa** (☏0363-21873; Jl Tirta Gangga; r incl breakfast from 175,000-250,000Rp; ☏), across from the Taman Tirta Gangga entrance. Book in advance. (☏0813 3840 2132, 0363-21873; bungbungbike adventure@gmail.com; Homestay Rijasa, Tirta Gangga; half-/full-day tours from 250,000/300,000Rp)

Pasir Putih

BEACH

10 ⊙ Map p120, E3

The most popular 'secret' beach on Bali, Pasir Putih (aka Dream Beach or Virgin Beach) is an idyllic white-sand beach whose name indeed means 'White Sand'. When we first visited in 2004, it was empty, save for a row of fishing boats at one end. Now it's an ongoing lab in seaside economic development.

Eating

Warung Enak

BALINESE $

11 ✕ Map p120, E1

Black rice pudding and other less-common local treats are the speciali-ties of this dead-simple and supertasty little eatery. It also does a fresh catch of the day and homemade ice cream. (☏0819 1567 9019; Jemeluk; mains from 50,000Rp; ☏9am-11pm)

Bali Asli

BALINESE $$

12 ✕ Map p120, E2

The green hills around Amlapura are some of east Bali's most beautiful, and Australian chef Penelope Williams takes full advantage of the vistas at this elegant restaurant and cook-ing school (1,000,000Rp). Produce sourced from her own garden is used for meals that explore the vibrancy of Balinese and Indonesian flavours. This may be the best *nasi campur* you'll ever have. (☏0822 3690 9215; www.baliasli.com.au; Jl Raya Glumpang, Glumpang;

Local Life
Chocolate Euphoria

Uforia (☏0363-21687; www.uforia chocolate.com; Jl Pura Mastima, Am-lapura; ☏9am-5pm, production tours 10am-4pm Mon-Wed Jun-Aug), 12km east of Candidasa, produces its own range of single-origin choco-late on-site using elements of per-maculture and organic ingredients. The tours offer fascinating insight into the production process; call ahead for bookings and directions. Each Saturday you can join a work-shop and make your own person-alised chocolate bars from scratch using a choice of ingredients.

Understand

Villages of East Bali

Find Bali's past amid evocative ruins in the former royal city of Semarapura. Follow the rivers coursing down the slopes on the Sidemen road to find vistas and valleys where you can try to invent new words for 'green'. On the coast there's groovy Padangbai and diving-hotspot Tulamben.

Pandangbai

There's a real traveller vibe about this little beach town. A compact seaside backpacker hub offers cheap places to stay and some fun cafes. The pace is slow, but should ambition strike there's good snorkelling and diving plus some easy walks.

Tulamben

The big attraction here sunk over 60 years ago. The wreck of the US cargo ship *Liberty* is among the best and most popular dive sites in Bali and this has given rise to an entire town based on scuba diving. Even snorkellers can easily swim out and enjoy the wreck and the coral. But if you don't plan to explore the briny waves, don't expect to hang out on the beach – the shore is made up of rather beautiful, large washed stones.

Semarapura

A tidy regional capital, Semarapura is a must-see for its fascinating Kertha Gosa (p122) complex, a relic of Bali from the time before the Dutch. Once the centre of Bali's most important kingdom, Semarapura is still commonly called by its old name, Klungkung.

Sideman

The Sideman region is getting more popular as a verdant escape every year, where a walk in any direction is a communion with nature. Winding through one of Bali's most beautiful river valleys, the road to Sidemen offers marvellous paddy-field scenery, a delightful rural character and extraordinary views of Gunung Agung (when the clouds permit).

The village is a centre for culture and arts, particularly *endek* cloth (used for traditional sarongs) and *songket* (silver- or gold-threaded cloth). **Pelangi Weaving** (📞0366-23012; Jl Soka 67; ⊗8am-6pm) has a couple of dozen employees busily creating downstairs, while upstairs you can relax with the Sidemen views from comfy chairs outside the showroom.

set menus 160,000-220,000Rp; ⊙10am-7pm; 🛜)

Vincent's INTERNATIONAL $$

13 Map p120, E3

One of east Bali's best restaurants, Vincent's has several distinct open-air rooms and a large and lovely rear garden with rattan furniture. The bar is an oasis of jazz. The menu combines excellent and inventive Balinese, fresh seafood and European dishes – don't miss the sambal selection. Thursday evenings there's live music. (📞0363-41368; www.vincentsbali.com; Jl Raya Candidasa; meals 60,000-150,000Rp; ⊙8am-11pm; 🛜)

Gianyar Night Market MARKET $

14 Map p120, A3

The sound of clattering cooking pots and the glare of bright lights add a frenetic and festive clamour to Gianyar's delicious night market, which any local will tell you has some of the best food in Bali. Scores of stalls set up each night in the centre and cook up a mouth-watering and jaw-dropping range of dishes. (Jl Ngurah Rai; dishes from 15,000Rp; ⊙5-11pm)

Topi Inn CAFE $

15 Map p120, D3

Juices, shakes and good coffees are served up throughout the day. Break-fasts are big and whatever is landed by the fishing boats outside the front door during the day is grilled by night. Refill your water bottle here for 2000Rp. It also has an atmospheric bamboo bar selling cheap beers. (📞0363-41424; Jl Silayukti; mains from 50,000Rp; ⊙7.30am-10pm)

Warung Ida BALINESE $

16 Map p120, C2

There's an actual Ida here and boy can she cook. The rest of the family serve up her special Indonesian dishes in a relaxed open-air setting. Come for a sunset Bintang and stay for a fine meal made with produce from the surrounding fields. It's on the main lane with accommodation. (📞0812 364 7384; mains from 40,000Rp)

Drinking

Sunshine BAR

17 Map p120, D3

In keeping with the local vibe, this barely there bar (most seats are outside on the pavement) serves simple grilled fish at night along with cold beer. The motto is 'light up our soul', which can be defined many ways, possibly through the impromptu jam sessions. (off Jl Silayukti; ⊙4pm-late)

Top Sights
Gili Trawangan

Getting There

⚓ **Boat** Blue Water Express (www.blue-water-express.com) leaves from Serangan and Padangbai. Rates are US$50 to US$60 one way; the trip takes about two hours.

Gili Trawangan's main drag boasts a glittering roster of lounge bars, hip hotels and cosmopolitan restaurants, mini-marts and dive schools. And yet, behind this glitzy facade, a bohemian character endures, with rickety warungs and reggae joints surviving between the cocktail tables. Fast boats have brought Gili T close to Bali and, for many, a night or two partying here, and enjoying its beautiful waters in between, is an essential part of their trip.

Don't Miss

Beaches

Gili T is ringed by the sort of powdery white sand people expect to find on Bali, but don't. On the east side of the island, where most of the action is, the sand is among the nicest in Indonesia. Think pearly white grains lapped by azure waters. Oh, yes.

Snorkelling

Surrounded by coral reefs and with easy beach access, Gili T offers superb snorkelling. If you enjoy swimming, there's no better feeling than exploring a reef without the burden of a tank on your back. You can start on any beach or go further out on one of many glass-bottomed boats. Besides the many fish, it's common to see sea turtles.

Diving

The Gili Islands are a superb dive destination as the marine life is plentiful and varied. Turtles and black- and white-tip reef sharks are common, and the macro life is excellent, with seahorses, pipefish and lots of crustaceans. Around the full moon large schools of bumphead parrotfish appear to feast on coral spawn; at other times manta rays cruise past dive sites.

Nightlife

Gili T morphs between rave central and boutique chic. Parties are held three nights a week (Monday, Wednesday and Friday), shifting between venues. DJs mix house, trance and increasingly some R 'n' B as the scene becomes more commercial. The island has more than a dozen great beachside drinking dens, ranging from sleek lounge bars to simple shacks.

☑ Top Tips

▶ Gili T's neighbours, Gili Meno and Gili Air, are much quieter, with a fraction of Gili T's nightlife.

▶ There are fly-by-night boat operators to the Gilis and there have been accidents; stick with the experienced companies.

▶ Gili Trawangan has ATMs.

▶ During Ramadan, nightlife is curtailed out of respect for local culture.

✗ Take a Break

Enjoying a prime beachfront location, **Scallywags** (☎ 0370-614 5301; www.scallywagsresort.com; meals 40,000-180,000Rp; ☺ 8am-10pm; ☎) offers casual yet stylish beach decor, polished glassware, switched-on service and superb cocktails. The dinner menu features tasty seafood – fresh lobster, tuna steaks, snapper and swordfish – and a great salad bar. The seafood barbecue lures many right in.

The Best of
Bali

Rice fields
MARTIN PUDDY / GETTY IMAGES ©

Best Walks
Ayung River Valley

🏃 The Walk

The wonders of the Ayung River (Sungai Ayung) are the focus of this outing, which may be close to Ubud but is a world away in terms of its pure tropical splendour. You'll walk in a lush valley past a rushing river amid impossibly green vistas. Along the way, you'll pass through an iconically typical village and cross through the old compound of one of Bali's greatest expat writers.

Start Campuan Bridge

Finish Campuan Bridge

Length 5km; five hours

🍴 Take a Break

There are no breaks in the valley! Bring plenty of water and assemble a picnic from a deli or cafe in Ubud. But towards the end of your walk, options for a pause abound. The cafes line up like a string of oases as you make your way blessedly downhill on Jl Raya Sanggingan.

Locals preparing for a festival in Penestanan

❶ Penestanan

From the Campuan Bridge, climb the steep concrete stairs opposite the Hotel Tjampuhan and walk west past rice fields and artists' studios in the village of **Penestanan**. You'll see more artists' studios and traditional family compounds. Look for the small temple that always graces a corner.

❷ Sayan

Now head north on a small road that curves around to **Sayan** and the **Sayan Terrace hotel**. This was the site of Colin McPhee's home in the1930s, as chronicled in his excellent book *A House in Bali* (available at island bookshops). He was one of the first Westerners to take a scholarly approach to documenting Bali's music and dance.

❸ Path into the Valley

Follow the downhill path before the gate to the hotel's rooms. It's steep and can be slippery, plus there are offshoots that can lead you astray; locals will help you for a tip of about 10,000Rp.

MANFRED GOTTSCHALK / GETTY IMAGES ©

Note that as you follow the river, you'll encounter farmers asking for money to cross their land; 5000Rp is a reasonable amount to give. There is no need to give money to any 'guides'.

❹ Ayung River Valley

Following the rough trails north, along the eastern side of the **Ayung**, you traverse steep slopes, cross paddy fields and pass irrigation canals through dense tropical jungle. You don't need to follow any specific trail as you head north along the river. Water plunges over huge boulders and eddies in cool-looking pools.

❺ Kedewatan

After about 1.5km of meandering through the river valley (take your time, wander about, see what you discover), you'll reach the finish point for white-water rafting trips that start further upriver. Under a dense canopy of trees, take a good but steep trail up to the main road at **Kedewatan**; head north then east about

1km along the main road into Ubud.

❻ Sanggingan

At **Sanggingan** the road curves 90 degrees due south and begins the long, gentle descent to the Campuan Bridge

where you started. Among the many cafes along here, pause for one of the famous martinis at Naughty Nuri's, or you can stop at the Neka Art Museum to see how artists portrayed many of the sights you've seen.

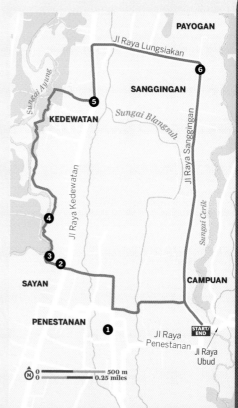

Best
Beaches

Bali is ringed with beaches, which is one of the reasons all those planes keep landing at the airport. They come in so many forms that there's virtually a beach for everyone. There's a reason that tourism started in Kuta: just look at that beach. It disappears in both directions and has ceaselessly crashing waves, which at their best are long aqua ribbons twisting into white.

A Beach for Any Mood

On Sundays Kuta Beach is thronged with locals; on any day massages and cheap beers from coolers are offered along the beach. Holidaymakers claim a part of the beach they like, make friends with the vendors and return to 'their' beach for the rest of their trip. From Seminyak north through Batubelig, Batu Bolong and on to Echo Beach, hipster hang-outs vie with posh clubs and humble beer vendors for business. South of the airport, the vast arid rock that is the Bukit Peninsula shelters a score of beaches hidden in small coves below the cliffs all the way to Ulu Watu. Coming closest to the white-sand cliché, these idylls are good for watching the world-class surfing offshore amid beautiful surrounds. Meanwhile, in Nusa Dua, Tanjung Benoa and Sanur, families frolic on mellow reef-sheltered beaches picked clean daily. East Bali has a swathe of seldom-visited volcanic black-sand beaches while Nusa Lembongan has beach guesthouses with awesome sunset views. Over on Gili T, the sand is white and lined with bars and clubs for a full-on party scene.

JOAKIMBKK / GETTY IMAGES ©

☑ Top Tips

▶ Although Bali's west-facing beaches from Echo Beach to Ulu Watu offer spectacular sunsets, east-facing ones like Sanur enjoy their own show as Nusa Lembongan (pictured above) and the islands glow pink offshore.

▶ Almost every beach has at least one vendor ready to pull a cold one out of the cooler.

Best for Hanging with Friends

Double Six Beach Fun mix of visitors and locals. (p27)

Gili Trawangan Those raves about the raves are just the start. (p126)

Seminyak Beach (p37)

Seminyak Beach Clubs and cafes great and humble dot the sand. (p37)

Batu Bolong The new hotspot with a cool, all-inclusive scene. (p51)

Balangan Beach Classic cove beach – worth the drive. (p69)

Kuta Beach The original beach still knows how to kick up some sand. (p26)

Echo Beach Gnarly surf action entertains the masses. (p51)

Padang Padang Beach Small enough to be one big scene on busy days. (p69)

Best for Families

Kuta Beach Surf schools. (p26)

Sanur Beach Kids will get their kicks in the gentle surf. (p85)

Batu Bolong Beach Where the cool kids of all ages hang out. (p51)

Best for Escaping

Bingin Beach Difficult access makes this the spot not to be spotted. (p69)

Pantai Klotek The sparkles in the black sand outnumber visitors a trillion to one. (p121)

Pantai Patra Jasa A hidden gem. (p26)

Best for Chilling Out

Balangan Beach This curving white-sand beach is ramshackle in

an endearing way and perfect for a snooze or booze. (p69)

Nusa Lembongan Beaches Little coves of dreamy sand you can walk between, plus fab swimming. (p90)

Best for Beach Dining

Jimbaran Famous for its array beachside restaurants serving grilled seafood. (p63)

Pasir Putih The coolest beach in East Bali with great cafes. (p123)

Pantai Lebih Admire fishing boats along the shore as you sample the catch of the day. (p121)

Best
Nightlife

The nightclub scene in Kuta, Legian and Seminyak is one of Bali's biggest draws. The partying starts at beachside bars at sunset and moves to an ever-changing line-up of bars and clubs. Bouncing from one to another all night long is a Bali tradition that guarantees you'll be overheated from the exertion, the music, the booze, the companionship or all of the above.

CHECHEW / GETTY IMAGES ©

☑ **Top Tips**

▸ Enjoying traditional Balinese nightlife may be the best memory of your trip: the dance performances in and around Ubud combine beauty, talent, drama and even comedy.

Nightlife for Every Taste

You can quaff an ice-cold Bintang at sandy-floored bars with the full tropical cliché. At the other end of the style spectrum there are several scenester clubs that may force you to spend just as much time prepping your look as actually partying. Mostly, however, nights on Bali are lacking in rules or pretension: on any night you can listen to live rock, dance salsa, see a drag show, cut shapes to a famous DJ set, win (or lose) a shot contest or just have a smashing good time with friends new and old.

Best Partying

Sky Garden Lounge Floor after floor of club and bar action fuelled by drink specials. (p32)

Gili Trawangan The entire island is renowned for its all-night raves. (p126)

Black Shores Cocktails, live bands and an easygoing vibe. (p55)

Best Stylish Drinking

Potato Head High-concept lounge and cocktails on the Seminyak sands. (p55)

Red Carpet Champagne Bar Ridiculously over-the-top for fizzy drinks and oysters. (p42)

Double-Six Rooftop Amazing sunsets and sleek, stylish surrounds. (p31)

La Favela Among Bali's most intriguing nightspots. (p41)

Best Live Music

Ryoshi Seminyak House of Jazz Regular local and international live acts. (p41)

Bali Joe Bali's best drag shows. (p42)

Pura Dalem Ubud An atmospheric place to witness traditional Balinese dance. (p114)

Best
Pampering

Whether it's a total fix for the mind, body and spirit, or simply the desire for some quick-fix serenity, many travellers to Bali can happily spend hours (sometimes days) being massaged, scrubbed, perfumed, pampered, bathed and blissed-out. Sometimes this happens on the beach or in a garden, other times in stylish, even lavish, surroundings.

Bliss in Every Flavour

Spas may be serious or they may seem frivolous; they can be found down little lanes and in the most exclusive hotels. Treatments are myriad, from the almost sensually relaxing to serious endeavours designed to purge your body and maybe your soul of toxins. You can lie back and enjoy or take active part; yoga is hugely popular. Happily the Balinese have just the right cultural background and disposition to enhance the experience.

Balinese Massage

Traditional Balinese massage techniques of stretching, long strokes, skin rolling and palm and thumb pressure result in a lowering of tension, improved blood flow and circulation, and an all-over feeling of calm. Traditional herbal treatments are popular.

Best Massage

Jari Menari Bali's renowned centre for serious massage. (p37)

Sundari Day Spa Organic massage oils set the mood at this day spa. (p51)

Best Pampering Spas

Prana Utterly lavish in its treatments and opulent in decor. (p38)

Jamu Traditional Spa Popular, serene and posh. (p28)

LUCKY BUSINESS / SHUTTERSTOCK ©

Jamu Wellness Elegant spa with a range of treatments. (p86)

Best Yoga

Yoga Barn The centre for all things yoga in Ubud. (p103)

Taksu Spa Combines yoga with spa treatments. (p108)

Power of Now Oasis Beachside yoga at dawn. (p86)

Best for Cleansing Your Body

Ubud Sari Health Resort Purge yourself of your excesses. (p108)

Best
Diving &
Snorkelling

The chance to stare down a 3m-long sunfish is reason enough to go diving here. These huge creatures are found at many spots around Bali, as are a huge variety of other fish and mammals, from parrotfish to whales. And snorkelling, at spots all around the islands, can be just as rewarding.

DUDAREV MIKHAIL / SHUTTERSTOCK ©

Diving Bali

With its warm water, extensive coral reefs and abundant marine life, Bali offers excellent diving adventures. Reliable dive schools and operators all around Bali's coasts can train complete beginners or arrange challenging trips that will satisfy most experienced divers. Out on Nusa Lembongan, you'll find top-notch dive operators who can take you to sites there and at neighbouring Nusa Penida – a world-class dive location. Gili T provides equally excellent opportunities. If you're not picky, you'll find all the equipment you need (the quality, size and age of the equipment can vary). If you provide your own, you can usually get a discount on your dive. Some small, easy-to-carry things to bring from home include protective gloves, spare mask straps, silicone lubricant and extra globes/bulbs for your torch/flashlight.

Snorkelling Bali

Snorkelling gear is available near all the most accessible spots, but if you've got space in your suitcase it's definitely worthwhile bringing your own and checking out some of the less-visited parts of the coasts. Anywhere there's a reef (apart from those with dangerously large waves), you won't go wrong slipping into the water to see what's swimming around.

☑ **Top Tips**

▶ Ask to see dive operators' certificates or certification cards – no reputable shop will be offended by this request. To guide certified divers on a reef dive, guides must hold at least 'rescue diver' or preferably 'dive master' qualifications.

▶ At a minimum, a dive boat should carry oxygen and a first-aid kit. A radio or mobile phone is also important.

Left: Snorkelling; Above Fish in a coral reef

Best Diving

Gili Trawangan Dive shops and spots abound on Gili T. Free-diving is popular here, and there are reefs in all directions. (p126)

Nusa Lembongan There are dozens of great sites here and at the two neighbouring islands. (p90)

World Diving Excellent Nusa Lembongan operator leads trips and offers certification. It also organises trips to the deep and challenging waters off nearby Nusa Penida. (p91)

Crystal Divers Sanur's top dive shop gives great lessons and organises trips. (p86)

Best Snorkelling

Gili Trawangan Wander into water teeming with fish and reefs right off the beach. (p126)

Nusa Lembongan Reefs and mangroves combine for many fine sites. (p90)

Padangbai Have fun snorkelling right off the beach. (p124)

Surya Water Sports Sanur's best water-sports shop offers boat trips for snorkellers. (p86)

Worth a Trip

Pulau Menjangan is Bali's best-known dive area and has a dozen superb dive sites. The diving is excellent – iconic tropical fish, soft corals, great visibility (usually), caves and a spectacular drop off. It's located on the northwest coast of the island and is best visited as part of an overnight jaunt to Pemuteran, which has resorts.

Best
Eating

Bali is a splendid destination for food. The local cuisine, whether truly Balinese or influenced by the rest of Indonesia and Asia, draws from the bounty of fresh local foods and is rich with spices and flavours. Savour this fare at roadside warungs (simple local cafes) or top-end restaurants, and for tastes further afield, you can choose from restaurants offering some of the best dining in the region.

KIBOKA / SHUTTERSTOCK ©

☑ **Top Tips**

▶ Every town of any size in Bali will have a *pasar malam* (night market), at which you can sample a vast range of fresh offerings from warungs and carts. Gianyar has a great one.

▶ If you happen to be drinking coffee with a Balinese person, don't be surprised if they tip the top layer of their coffee on the ground. This is an age-old protection against evil spirits.

Balinese Cuisine

Food, glorious food – or should that be food, laborious food? Balinese cooking is a time-consuming activity, but no effort at all is required to enjoy the results. That part is one of the best things about travelling around Bali: the sheer variety and quality of the local cuisine will have your taste buds dancing all the way to the next warung.

The fragrant aromas of Balinese cooking will taunt you wherever you go. Even in your average village compound, the finest food is prepared fresh every day. Women go to their local marketplace first thing in the morning to buy whatever produce has been brought from the farms overnight. They cook enough to last all day, diligently roasting the coconut until the smoky sweetness kisses your nose, painstakingly and grinding the spices to form the perfect *base* (paste). The dishes are covered on a table or stored in a glass cabinet for family members to serve themselves throughout the day.

Markets

There's no better place to get acquainted with Balinese cuisine than the local market. But it's not for late sleepers. The best time to go is around 6am to 7am. The atmosphere is lively and colourful with baskets loaded with fresh fruits, vegetables, flowers, spices, and varieties of red, black and white rice.

Left: Coffee; Above: Balinese cuisine

Best Top End

Locavore Ubud's world-class temple to farm-to-table seasonal eating; book far in advance. (p110)

Sardine Amid the south Bali hubbub, an oasis set on a private rice field; exquisite seafood, great bar. (p54)

Mozaic A long-time trendsetter of fine dining in a beautiful Ubud garden. (p112)

Bumbu Bali Exquisite set menus. (p80)

Best Indonesian

Nasi Ayam Kedewatan The place for *sate lilit* (minced fish, chicken or pork satay) in a simple open-front dining room on the edge of Ubud. (p112)

Warung Sulawesi Delicious dishes from across the archipelago, served in a shady family courtyard. (p54)

Warung Eny A visitor favourite; if you like what you eat, they'll show you how to cook it. (p54)

Warung Teges Great Balinese fare loved by locals, just south of Ubud. (p111)

Warung Ida Ida and her family serve up local specialities. (p125)

Best International

Pica South American dishes from an open kitchen in Ubud? Yes, and the results delight. (p111)

Warung Goûthé Bali's best casual French lunch; daily specials are just that. (p53)

Take Fresh Balinese seafood stars in Japanese classics. (p28)

Sisterfields Classic and creative Aussie plates. (p38)

Best Markets

Pasar Badung At Denpasar's huge market you'll find every kind of food grown on Bali. (p97)

Jimbaran Fish Market As well as its legendary fish market, Jimbaran has a morning market of fruit and vegetables. (p63)

Semarapura Market Offers an all-day bounty. (p121)

Gianyar Night Market Have fun just strolling, browsing and choosing. (p125)

Best
Surfing

Listen to the surfer tongues: Australian, American, Italian, Dutch, Japanese, Balinese (yes, lots of Balinese!) and many more are heard. People from all over the world come to Bali to surf, which shouldn't surprise anyone. Bali's surf breaks are legendary and they are many. The series off Ulu Watu are among the world's best.

WESTEND61 / GETTY IMAGES ©

Where to Surf

Swells come from the Indian Ocean, so the surf is on the southern side of the island and, strangely, on the northwest coast of Nusa Lembongan, where the swell funnels into the strait between there and the Bali coast.

In the dry season (around April to September), the west coast has the best breaks, with the trade winds coming in from the southeast; this is also when Nusa Lembongan is at its best. In the wet season, surf the eastern side of the island, from Nusa Dua around to Padangbai. If there's a north wind – or no wind at all – there are also a couple of breaks on the south coast of the Bukit Peninsula.

Note that the best breaks almost always have good beaches of the same name.

To reach the breaks, many will rent a motorbike with a surfboard rack while others will hire a surfboard-carrying-capable car with a driver. Either option is easily accomplished.

Best Surf Breaks

Kuta Beach Bali's original surf beach is still a winner. (p26)

Batu Bolong Light sand, many surfers and a cool party scene. (p51)

Bingin Close to cheap surfer lodgings, this isolated beach is worth the climb down a cliff. (p72)

Double Six Beach Great mix of tourists and locals. (p27)

Impossibles Challenging outside reef break. (p72)

Echo Beach Wild waves and plenty of spectators. (p51)

Ulu Watu Bali's best surf breaks are truly incredible. (p71)

Balangan Right off a great beach with fun cafes. (p72)

Nusa Lembongan Three famous breaks are right off Jungutbatu Beach. (p90)

Best Surf Schools

Pro Surf School Long-running school that can get almost anyone surfing. (p28)

Rip Curl School of Surf Part of an entire surfing lifestyle empire. (p28)

Surf Goddess Runs surf holidays for women. (p38)

Best
For Kids

Bali is a good place for kids. There's lots of kid-friendly fun to be had and the locals are especially enamoured of pint-sized visitors. Cool things to do include a) beaches, b) pools – almost every hotel has one, c) mysterious temples, d) monkeys, e) tourist parks geared to kids, f) ocean adventures like snorkelling, and a lot more.

JANGLA / SHUTTERSTOCK ©

The Balinese & Children

Children are a social asset when you travel in Bali, and people will display great interest in any Western child they meet. You will have to learn your child's age and sex in Bahasa Indonesia – *bulan* is month, *tahun* is year, *laki-laki* is boy and *perempuan* is girl. You should also make polite enquiries about the other person's children, present or absent.

☑ **Top Tips**

▶ Look for beach vendors selling kites; huge breezy fun.

▶ Given the ongoing rabies crisis in Bali, be sure to keep children away from stray dogs.

Best Watery Fun

Rip Curl School of Surf Popular surf school with kids' programs. (p28)

Benoa Marine Recreation Oodles of aquatic fun. (p81)

Sanur Beach Mellow waters and lots of clean sand. (p85)

Surya Water Sports Tons of cool reasons to get wet. (p86)

Mushroom Bay Sheltered beach on Nusa

Lembongan with water sports. (p91)

Best Amusement Parks

Canggu Club Has a new slide-filled water park. (p52)

Waterbom Park A wet, wild and watery kingdom. (p27)

Best Random Fun

Sacred Monkey Forest Sanctuary Indiana

Jones–like temples in a forest filled with monkeys. (p106)

Pura Luhur Ulu Watu An ancient temple with sea views and, yes, monkeys. (p71)

JJ Bali Button Millions of cool buttons. (p57)

Bali Kite Festival Ginormous kites roaring overhead. (p86)

Best
Shopping

DIMA FADEEV / SHUTTERSTOCK ©

Bali's shops could occupy days of your holiday. Designer boutiques (Bali has a thriving fashion industry), slick galleries, wholesale emporiums and family-run workshops are just some of the choices. The shopping scene is like a form of primordial soup. New boutiques appear, old ones vanish, some change into something else while others move up the food chain.

Bargaining

Bargaining can be an enjoyable part of shopping in Bali. Try following these steps:

▶ Have some idea of the item's worth.

▶ Establish a starting price – ask the seller for their price.

▶ Your first offer can be from one-third to two-thirds of that price.

▶ If you don't like the price, walk – the vendor may go lower.

▶ When you name a price, you're committed – you must buy if your offer is accepted.

☑ **Top Tips**

▶ Much of Kuta, Legian and certain euphemistically named 'art markets' in Ubud, Seminyak and elsewhere are filled with junk that's not even made on Bali.

▶ The top-selling souvenir is the penis-shaped bottle opener; the irony is that the imagery actually has deep roots in Balinese beliefs (penises abound in old temple carvings).

Left: Woodcarvers; Above: Cane souvenirs in Ubud

Best Clothes

Rumble Locally designed streetwear. (p114)

Milo's Silken treasures from a local legend. (p44)

Prisoners of St Petersburg Threads from Bali's freshest designers. (p43)

Bamboo Blonde The cure for terminal frump. (p44)

Thaikila Balinese-made bikinis, with a soupçon of French style. (p45)

Best for Browsing

JJ Bali Button Fun for the whole family; buttons pack easily too. (p57)

Ganesha Bookshop Bali's best bookshop has carefully chosen selections. (p89)

Pasar Badung Bali's large central market has it all. (p97)

Theatre Art Gallery Vintage and replica traditional puppets. (p44)

Best Homewares

Hobo Clever housewares designed and made on Bali. (p57)

Bathe Fun stuff for the house that smells good. (p56)

Souq Inspired by the Middle East, designed in Bali. (p43)

Best Gifts & Souvenirs

Threads of Life Indonesian Textile Arts Center Handmade traditional Bali fabrics. (p116)

Ashitaba Beautiful, ornate rattan work. (p45)

Joger A Bali retail legend. (p33)

UpCycle Hunt for upcycled treasures. (p33)

Best for Surfers

Drifter High-end surfwear. (p44)

Luke Studer Renowned south Bali board shaper. (p32)

Dylan Board Store Custom boards by renowned surfer Dylan Longbottom. (p57)

Surfer Girl Another of Bali's iconic surf brands. (p33)

Best
LGBT Bali

Bali easily ranks as one of the world's most tolerant LGBT travel destinations. Much of this stems from the beliefs and attitudes ingrained in the Balinese. People are accepted as they are, judging others is considered extremely rude and there's a limited macho culture where masculinity is easily threatened.

AGUNG PARAMESWARA / STRINGER / GETTY IMAGES ©

LGBT Travellers & the Balinese

Bali is a popular spot for LGBT travellers owing to the many ways it caters to a rainbow of visitors. There is a large gay and lesbian expat community and many own businesses that that – if not gay-specific – are very gay-friendly. In south Bali and Ubud, couples have few concerns, beyond remembering that the Balinese are quite modest. Otherwise, there's a rollicking strip of very-gay-friendly nightclubs in the heart of Seminyak, although there's no part of Bali any LGBT person should avoid.

Having said that, gay travellers in Bali (and Indonesia) should follow the same precautions as straight travellers: avoid public displays of affection.

One of the converse effects about having gay life so much a part of life on Bali is that there are relatively few 'gay' places, although many bars and clubs of Seminyak's Jl Abimanyu form a nexus of gay Bali.

Best LGBT Nightlife

Bali Joe Fab drag shows draw a mixed crowd; several other clubs are nearby. (p42)

Bottoms Up Dancers, drag shows and more. (p43)

☑ Top Tips

▶ Homosexual behaviour is not illegal on Bali.

▶ Gay men in Indonesia are referred to as homo or gay; lesbians are *lesbi*.

▶ Indonesia's community of transvestite and transsexual *waria* has always had a very public profile.

▶ GAYa Nusantara (www.gayanusantara.or.id) has a very useful website that covers local LGBT issues.

▶ Bali's gay organisation is Gaya Dewata (www.gayadewata.com).

Best
Festivals &
Ceremonies

MAZZZUR / GETTY IMAGES ©

There you are sipping a coffee at a cafe in, say, Seminyak or Ubud, when there's a crash of the gamelan and traffic screeches to a halt as a crowd of elegantly dressed people come flying by bearing pyramids of fruit, tasselled parasols and a furred, masked Barong (mythical lion-dog creature) or two. It's a temple procession, disappearing as suddenly as it appeared, leaving no more than a fleeting sparkle of gold and white silk and hibiscus petals in its wake. Dozens occur daily across Bali.

Temple Festivals

Each of the thousands of temples on the island has a 'temple birthday' known as an *odalan*. These are celebrated once every Balinese year of 210 days or every 354 to 356 days on the *caka* calendar (yes, it's bewildering – there are priests who do nothing but try to sort out the calendar).

Best Special Days

Nyepi The year's most special day is marked by total inactivity – to convince evil spirits that Bali is uninhabited, so they'll leave the island alone. The night before, huge papier-mâché monsters (*ogoh-ogoh*) go up in flames. You'll see these built by enthusiastic locals in communities islandwide in the weeks before. Held in March or early April.

Galungan One of Bali's major festivals. During a 10-day period, all the gods come down to earth for the festivities, which celebrate the death of a legendary tyrant called Mayadenawa. Barong prance from temple to temple and village to village (many of these processions consist entirely of children), and locals rejoice with feasts and visits to families.

☑ **Top Tips**

▶ Ask any locals you meet what *odalan* (temple festivals) are happening. Seeing one will be a highlight of your trip, particularly if it is at a major temple. Foreigners are welcome to watch the festivities, but be unobtrusive and dress modestly.

Kuningan Culmination of Galungan, when the Balinese say thanks and goodbye to the gods. You'll see large temple ceremonies across the island – and likely be caught in long traffic queues as a result. Abandon your vehicle and join the scene. On beaches, families dressed spotlessly in white look for purification from the ocean's waters.

Best
Art

Until visitors arrived in great numbers, the acts of painting or carving were purely to decorate temples and shrines as well as enrich ceremonies. Today, with galleries and craft shops everywhere, paintings are stacked up on gallery floors and you may trip over carvings in both stone and wood. Amid the tat, however, you will find a great deal of beautiful work.

Painting

Balinese painting is the art form most influenced by Western ideas. Ubud's art museums and galleries have a range of beautiful paintings. Styles range from abstract works of incredible colour to beautiful and evocative representations – some highly idealised – of island life.

Crafts

Bali is a showroom for crafts from around Indonesia. The nicer tourist shops will sell puppets and batiks from Java; ikat garments from Sumba, Sumbawa and Flores; and textiles and woodcarvings from Bali, Lombok and Kalimantan. Carving was traditionally done for temples and the Balinese are experts, with works – such as a frog using a leaf as an umbrella – often showing their sense of humour.

JOHN ELK III / GETTY IMAGES ©

☑ **Top Tips**

▶ Bali's arts and crafts originated in honouring fertility of the land and Dewi Sri, the rice goddess.

▶ Batubulan, on the main road from south Bali to Ubud, is a major stone-carving centre. Figures line both sides of the road, and carvers can be seen in action in the many workshops.

Best Museums & Galleries

Museum Le Mayeur House and gallery of one of Bali's most influential painters. (p85)

Agung Rai Museum of Art Excellent private museum in Ubud. (p107; pictured above)

Museum Puri Lukisan A great history of Balinese art. (p106)

Pasifika Museum Large museum with fine works from Bali and the region. (p79)

Neka Art Museum Has paintings by many of the local greats. (p106)

Museum Negeri Propinsi Bali The island's main museum has art from the ages. (p95)

Survival Guide

Survival Guide

Before You Go

When to Go

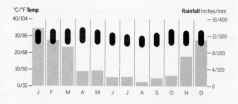

High Season (Jul, Aug & Dec) Accommodation rates up by 50% or more. Many hotels are booked far ahead; the best restaurants need to be booked in advance. Christmas and New Year are expensive and crowded.

Shoulder (May, Jun & Sep) The best weather (drier, less humid). Good room deals and last-minute bookings are possible. Best time for many activities including diving.

Low Season (Jan–Apr, Oct & Nov) Deals everywhere, good airfares. Rainy season – though rainfall is never excessive. Can do most activities.

Book Your Stay

➡ **The Basics** Bali has a huge range of great-value accommodation for any budget. If visiting in the peak periods of August and Christmas, book three or more months ahead.

➡ **Resorts** Bali has some of the world's best resorts and at prices that would be a bargain elsewhere. You can be on the beach or nestled in a lush mountain valley.

➡ **Villas** Enjoy a sybaritic escape and a private pool.

➡ **Hotels** Many of Bali's hundreds of hotels are located near the action and offer good deals.

➡ **Homestays & Guesthouses** Bali's family-run accommodation is comfortable and puts you right in the middle of fascinating local life.

Useful Websites
Bali Private Villas (www.baliprivatevillas.com)

Handles a a variety of top-end villas.

Bali Ultimate Villas (www.baliultimatevillas. net) A villa agent that also offers wedding services.

JED (www.jed.or.id) Arrange a village stay through the Village Eco-tourism Network.

Lonely Planet (www. lonelyplanet.com/indo nesia/bali) Destination information, hotel bookings, traveller forum and more.

Best Budget
Pondok Baruna (www. pondokbaruna.com) Associated with local diver operator World Diving, this place offers fantastic rooms with terraces facing the ocean at Jungutbatu Beach, Nusa Lembongan.

Kuta Bed & Breakfast (kutabnb@gmail.com) Nine comfortable rooms in an excellent guesthouse right across from Bemo Corner – it has all the basics. It's a 10-minute walk from the beach and a 10-minute ride from the airport. It has a wonderful rooftop with views over the Kuta skyline; nightlife is close too.

Khrisna Home Stay (pinpinaryadi@yahoo. com) This wonderful seven-room homestay is surrounded by all-organic trees and plants growing guava, bananas, passion fruit, papaya, oranges and more. Needless to say, breakfasts are excellent. The rooms are comfortable (with terraces) and the owners lovely.

Padma Ubud (www. padmaubud.com) Twelve very private bungalows in a tropical garden with a pool. Rooms are decorated with local crafts and the modern outdoor bathrooms have hot water.

Best Midrange
Matahari Cottages (www.matahariubud. com) This whimsical Ubud guesthouse has 15 flamboyant, themed rooms, including the 'Batavia Princess' and the 'Indian Pasha'. The library is a vision out of a 1920s fantasy. It also boasts a self-proclaimed 'jungle jacuzzi', an upscale way to replicate the old Bali tradition of river-bathing. There's a multicourse breakfast and high tea elaborately served on silver.

Temple Lodge (www. thetemplelodge.com) 'Artsy and beautiful' just begins to describe this collection of huts and cottages made from thatch, driftwood and other natural materials. Each sits on a jutting shelf on the cliffs above the surf breaks, and there are superb views from the infinity pool and some of the seven units.

Rock'n Reef (www. rock-n-reef.com) Six bungalows are built into the rocks on Impossibles Beach, with stunning views of the ocean directly in front. Each has a rustic, artful design with natural materials such as stucco and driftwood. There are private balconies and sunny decks. An all-day cafe offers simple Indonesian meals.

Swasti Eco Cottages (www.baliswasti.com) A five-minute walk from the south entrance to the Monkey Forest, this compound has large grounds that feature an organic garden (produce is used in the cafe). Some rooms are in simple two-storey blocks; others are in vintage traditional houses brought here from across Indonesia. Its green cred out-Ubuds Ubud.

Best Top End

Como Uma Ubud (www.comohotels.com) One of Ubud's most attractive properties, the 46 rooms here come in a variety of sizes but all have a relaxed naturalistic style that goes well with the gorgeous views over the gardens and the river valley beyond. Service and amenities are superb.

Alila Villas Uluwatu (www.alilahotels.com/uluwatu) Visually stunning, this vast resort has an artful contemporary style that is at once light and airy while still conveying a sense of luxury. The 85-unit Alila offers gracious service in a setting where the blue of the ocean contrasts with the green of the surrounding (hotel-tended) rice fields. It's 2km off Jl Ulu Watu.

Hotel Tugu Bali (www.tuguhotels.com) Right at Batu Bolong Beach, this exquisite hotel blurs the boundaries between accommodation and a museum-gallery, especially the Walter Spies and Le Mayeur Pavilions,

where memorabilia from the artists' lives decorates the rooms. There's a spa and a high-style beachfront bar, Ji.

Amankila (www.amankila.com) One of Bali's best resorts, the Amankila is perched along the jutting cliffs in east Bali. About 5.6km beyond the Padangbai turn-off and 500m past the road to Manggis, a discreetly marked side road leads to the hotel. It features an isolated seaside location with views to Nusa Penida.

Arriving in Bali

Ngurah Rai International Airport

➡ Ngurah Rai International Airport (http://bali-airport.com), just south of Kuta, is the only airport in Bali. It is sometimes referred to internationally as Denpasar or on some internet flight-booking sites as Bali.

➡ International airlines flying to and from Bali have myriad flights to Australia and Asian capitals. The

present runway is too short for planes flying nonstop to/from Europe.

➡ Bali's current airport terminal opened in 2013. Unfortunately, it has many problems including a serpentine layout, long queues at immigration and customs, and non-functioning escalators.

➡ From here, a taxi to Kuta is 80,000Rp, to Seminyak it's 130,000Rp and to Ubud it's 300,000Rp.

Getting Around

Car & Driver

➡ An excellent way to travel anywhere around Bali is by hired vehicle; if you're part of a group, it can make sound economic sense as well.

➡ Costs for a full day should average 500,000Rp to 800,000Rp.

➡ It's easy to arrange a charter: just listen for one of the frequent offers of 'transport?' in the streets around the tourist centres. Approach a driver yourself, ask at your hotel, or seek recommendations from other travellers.

➡ On the road, buy the driver lunch (they'll want to eat elsewhere, so give them 20,000Rp) and offer snacks and drinks.

Taxi

➡ Metered taxis are common in south Bali and Denpasar (but not Ubud). They are essential for getting around and you can usually flag one down in busy areas.

➡ The best taxi company by far is **Blue Bird Taxi** (☎0361-701111; www. bluebirdgroup.com), which uses blue vehicles with a light on the roof bearing a stylised bluebird. Watch out for myriad fakes – look for 'Blue Bird' over the windscreen and the phone number. Also has a slick app.

➡ Avoid any taxis where the driver won't use a meter.

Car & Motorbike

➡ Renting a car or motorbike can open up Bali for exploration – and can also leave you counting the minutes until you return it; driving conditions can be harrowing, and in south Bali traffic is often awful.

➡ Any place you stay will be able to help you organise rental. Rates are around 50,000Rp per day.

Bicycle

➡ There are plenty of bicycles for rent in the tourist areas, but many are in poor condition. Ask at your accommodation. Prices are from 30,000Rp per day.

Boat

➡ Fast boats link Bali and nearby islands.

➡ Boats are unregulated and there have been accidents. Go with established companies and confirm there are life boats and easily accessed life preservers before departure.

Essential Information

Business Hours

Restaurants & cafes 8am to 10pm daily

Shops & services catering to visitors 9am to 8pm or later daily

Electricity

Type C
220V/50Hz

Type F
230V/50Hz

Health

➡ Tap water in Bali is never safe to drink.

➡ Bottled water is generally safe but check the seal is intact when purchasing. Look for places that allow you to refill containers, thus cutting down on landfill.

➡ Avoid fresh juices outside of tourist restaurants and cafes.

➡ In south Bali and Ubud there are clinics catering to tourists, and just about any hotel can put you in touch with an English-speaking doctor.

➡ For serious conditions go to the costly private clinic **BIMC** (☏0361-300 0911, 0361-761263; www. bimcbali.com; Jl Ngurah Rai 100X; ⏱24hr), which caters mainly to tourists and expats.

➡ Ensure that you have travel insurance that covers medical evacuation. Some policies exclude 'dangerous activities,' which can include scuba diving, renting a local motorcycle and even trekking.

➡ Dengue fever is a problem; wear mosquito repellents that contain DEET. Choose accommodation with screens and fans (if not air-conditioned).

➡ Rabies is a major problem; if you are bitten or come into contact with a stray animal, seek medical attention immediately as rabies is fatal. Watch children closely.

➡ There are ongoing reports of injuries and deaths among tourists and locals due to *arak* (local spirits that should be distilled from palm or cane sugar) being adulterated with methanol, a poisonous form of alcohol. Although *arak* is a popular drink, it should be avoided outside established restaurants and cafes.

➡ Traveller's diarrhoea (aka Bali belly) is common. Stay well hydrated – rehydration solutions such as Gastrolyte are the best for this – and if it doesn't improve within 24 hours, consider antibiotics.

➡ Bali is hot and humid throughout the year; avoid dehydration and excessive activity in the heat. Wear strong sunscreen, a hat and sunglasses.

Money

➡ The unit of currency is the rupiah (Rp).

➡ ATMs are common and it's easy to exchange money.

➡ Credit cards are accepted at more expensive establishments.

➡ US dollars are by far the easiest to exchange.

ATMs

➡ There are ATMs all over Bali, with the notable exception of Nusa Lembongan.

➡ Most ATMs return your card after dispensing cash, so it's easy to forget your card.

Tipping

➡ Tipping a set percentage is not expected in Bali, but if the service is good, it's appropriate to leave at least 5000Rp or 10% or more.

➡ Hand cash directly to individuals (taxi drivers, porters, people giving you a massage, bringing you a beer at the beach etc) to recognise their service; 5000Rp to 10,000Rp or 10% to 20% of the total fee is generous.

➡ Most midrange and all top-end hotels and restaurants add 21% to the bill for tax and service (called 'plus plus').

Money Changers

➡ Find out the going exchange rate online. Know that anyone offering a better rate or claiming to charge no fees or commissions will need to make a profit through other means.

→ Stick to banks, airport exchange counters or large and reputable operations such as the Central Kuta Money Exchange (www.central kutabali.com), which has locations across south Bali and Ubud.

Public Holidays

The following holidays are celebrated throughout Indonesia. Many of the dates change according to the phase of the moon (not by month) or by religious calendar, so they are estimates only.

Tahun Baru Masehi (New Year's Day) 1 January

Tahun Baru Imlek (Chinese New Year) Late January to early February

Wafat Yesus Kristus (Good Friday) Late March or early April

Hari Buruh (Labour Day) 1 May

Hari Waisak (Buddha's birth, enlightenment and death) May

Kenaikan Yesus Kristus (Ascension of Christ) May

Hari Proklamasi Ke-merdekaan (Independ-ence Day) 17 August

Hari Natal (Christmas Day) 25 December

Safe Travel

→ Violent crime is uncom-mon, but bag-snatching, pickpocketing and theft from rooms and parked cars are all on the increase.

→ Don't take drugs to Bali nor buy any while there. Penalties are severe. Kuta is filled with cops posing as dealers.

→ Avoid beaches and the ocean around streams running into the water af-ter rain because all sorts of unsavoury matter may be present.

→ Be careful when walk-ing on the pavement; gaping holes can cause severe injury. Carry a torch (flashlight) at night.

→ Many visitors regard hawkers and touts as the number one annoyance in Bali, but ultimately they're just people try-ing to make a living. If you're not interested in purchasing their wares, completely ignore them – a polite *tidak* (no) actually encourages them.

Telephone

→ Cheap local SIM cards (from 5000Rp with no

calling credit) are sold everywhere and easily topped up with credit.

→ Data speeds of 3G and faster are the norm across Bali.

→ Any modern mobile phone will work.

Toilets

→ Western-style toilets are almost universal in tourist areas.

→ During the day, look for a cafe or hotel and smile (public toilets only exist at some major sights).

Travellers with Disabilities

→ Indonesia has very little supportive legislation or special programs for people with disabilities, and it's a difficult destina-tion for those with limited mobility.

→ Download Lonely Plan-et's free Accessible Travel guide from http://lptravel. to/AccessibleTravel.

Visas

→ Citizens of most coun-tries can receive a 30-day visa for free upon arrival. Note that this visa cannot be extended.

Index

See also separate subindexes for:

⊗ **Eating p156**

☻ **Drinking p157**

✪ Entertainment p157

🔒 **Shopping p157**

🔒 Sports & Activities p158

Sights 000
Map Pages **000**

Behind the Scenes

Send Us Your Feedback

We love to hear from travellers – your comments help make our books better. We read every word, and we guarantee that your feedback goes straight to the authors. Visit **lonelyplanet.com/contact** to submit your updates and suggestions.

Note: We may edit, reproduce and incorporate your comments in Lonely Planet products such as guidebooks, websites and digital products, so let us know if you don't want your comments reproduced or your name acknowledged. For a copy of our privacy policy visit lonelyplanet.com/privacy.

Our Readers

Many thanks to the travellers who wrote to us with helpful hints, useful advice and interesting anecdotes:

Jenny Borsuk, Agustina Calvo, Mariona Gelabert, Mick Green, Jochem van Iterson, Tina Porsbak, Torben Wuertz

Rucina, Neal, Jenny & Phillip, Ani, Nicoline, Eliot Cohen, Pascal & Pika and many more including Samuel L Bronkowitz. Huge thanks to Amy, the rest of the family and Charlie, who never once ate my shoes. Love to Alexis Ver Berkmoes, we'll always have Bali, Lada Warung or not.

Ryan's Thanks

Many thanks to friends like Patticakes, Ibu Cat, Hanafi, Stuart, Suzanne,

Acknowledgements

Cover photograph: Rice field, Martin Puddy/Getty Images ©

This Book

This 5th edition of Lonely Planet's *Pocket Bali* guidebook was curated by Imogen Bannister and researched and written by Ryan Ver Berkmoes. The previous two editions were also written by Ryan. This guidebook was produced by the following:

Destination Editors Sarah Reid, Dora Whitaker

Product Editors Kathryn Rowan, Sandie Kestell

Senior Cartographer Julie Sheridan

Book Designer Wibowo Rusli

Assisting Editors Janet Austin, Judith Bamber, Melanie Dankel, Gabrielle Innes, Kellie Langdon, Fionnuala Twomey, Simon Williamson

Cartographer Valentina Kremenchutskaya

Cover Researcher Naomi Parker

Thanks to Hannah Cartmel, Grace Dobell, Bruce Evans, Shona Gray, Alison Lyall, Catherine Naghten, Kirsten Rawlings

Our Writers

Ryan Ver Berkmoes

Ryan Ver Berkmoes has written more than 110 guide-books for Lonely Planet. He grew up in Santa Cruz, California, which he left at age 17 for college in the Midwest, where he first discovered snow. All joy of this novelty soon wore off. Since then he has been travelling the world, both for pleasure and for work – which are often indistinguishable. Read more at ryanverberkmoes. com and @ryanvb.

Published by Lonely Planet Global Limited
CRN 554153
5th edition – Jul 2017
ISBN 978 1 78657 544 9
© Lonely Planet 2017 Photographs © as indicated 2017
10 9 8 7 6 5 4 3 2 1
Printed in Malaysia

Although the authors and Lonely Planet have taken all reasonable care in preparing this book, we make no warranty about the accuracy or completeness of its content and, to the maximum extent permitted, disclaim all liability arising from its use.